Stratification and Inequality Series
The Center for the Study of Social Stratification and Inequality,
Tohoku University, Japan
Volume 6

Gender and Career in Japan

Stratification and Inequality Series
The Center for the Study of Social Stratification and Inequality,
Tohoku University, Japan

Inequality amid Affluence: Social Stratification in Japan
Junsuke Hara and Kazuo Seiyama

Intentional Social Change: A Rational Choice Theory
Yoshimichi Sato

Constructing Civil Society in Japan: Voices of Environmental Movements
Koichi Hasegawa

Deciphering Stratification and Inequality: Japan and beyond
Yoshimichi Sato

Social Justice in Japan: Concepts, Theories and Paradigms
Ken-ichi Ohbuchi

Gender and Career in Japan
Atsuko Suzuki

Stratification and Inequality Series
The Center for the Study of Social Stratification and Inequality,
Tohoku University, Japan
Volume 6

Gender and Career in Japan

Edited by
Atsuko Suzuki

Translated by
Leonie R. Stickland

This English edition first published in 2007 by
Trans Pacific Press, PO Box 120, Rosanna, Melbourne, Victoria 3084, Australia
Telephone: +61 (0)3-9459-3021 Fax: +61 (0)3-9457-5923
Email: tpp.mail@gmail.com
Web: http://www.transpacificpress.com

Copyright © Trans Pacific Press 2007

Designed and set by digital environs, Melbourne. http://www.digitalenvirons.com

Printed by BPA Print Group, Burwood, Victoria, Australia

Distributors

Australia and New Zealand
UNIREPS
University of New South Wales
Sydney, NSW 2052
Australia
Telephone: +61(0)2-9664-0999
Fax: +61(0)2-9664-5420
Email: info.press@unsw.edu.au
Web: http://www.unireps.com.au

USA and Canada
International Specialized Book
Services (ISBS)
920 NE 58th Avenue, Suite 300
Portland, Oregon 97213-3786
USA
Telephone: (800) 944-6190
Fax: (503) 280-8832
Email: orders@isbs.com
Web: http://www.isbs.com

Asia and the Pacific
Kinokuniya Company Ltd.

Head office:
Shin-Mizonokuchi Bldg. 2F
5-7 Hisamoto 3-chome
Takatsu-ku, Kawasaki 213-8506
Japan
Telephone: +81(0)44-874-9642
Fax: +81(0)44-829-1025
Email: bkimp@kinokuniya.co.jp
Web: www.kinokuniya.co.jp

Asia-Pacific office:
Kinokuniya Book Stores of Singapore Pte., Ltd.
391B Orchard Road #13-06/07/08
Ngee Ann City Tower B
Singapore 238874
Telephone: +65-6276-5558
Fax: +65-6276-5570
Email: SSO@kinokuniya.co.jp

All rights reserved. No production of any part of this book may take place without the written permission of Trans Pacific Press.

ISBN 978-1-876843-63-2 (Hardback)
ISBN 978-1-876843-57-1 (Paperback)

The National Library of Australia Cataloguing-in-Publication entry

Gender and career in Japan.

Bibliography.
Includes index.
ISBN 9781876843632 (hbk.)
ISBN 9781876843571 (pbk.)

1. Sex discrimination in employment – Japan. 2. Sexual division of labor – Japan. 3. Women – Employment – Japan. 4. Men – Employment – Japan. 5. Labor market – Japan. 6. Career development – Japan. I. Suzuki, Atsuko.

306.3615

Contents

Figures   *vi*
Tables   *viii*
Preface   *Atsuko Suzuki*   *x*
Acknowledgements   *xiv*
List of Contributors   *xv*

1 Introduction: Micro–Macro Dynamics *Atsuko Suzuki*   1
2 Work, Child-rearing and Gender: Psychological Distress in Women with Pre-schooler Children in Japan *Akihide Inaba*   33
3 Gender and Leadership Effectiveness in the Workplace *Kiriko Sakata*   58
4 Education, Employment and Gender Ideology *Kunihiro Kimura*   84
5 Job Discontinuation and Return to the Workforce after First Childbirth: The Case of Young Married Korean Women *Jikyung Kim*   110

Notes   145
References   150
Index   165

Figures

1.1 Parental time spent with children: 6-country comparison   16
1.2 Transitions in the labour-force participation rate in Japan: 1975 and 2005   18
1.3 Ratio of women among employees in managerial positions: 8-country comparison   22
2.1 Mean scores of psychological distress by youngest child's age and women's employment status (NFRJ98)   46
2.2 Mean scores of psychological distress by youngest child's age and women's employment status (NFRJ03)   46
3.1 The hypothetical model of gender-difference in leadership effectiveness   74
3.2 The interaction effect of bosses' gender, pressure P and M behaviour on performance norm scores   80
4.1 Associations among educational attainment, employment, and gender ideology for Japanese married women   85
4.2 Employment status of married women ('mothers' aged 36–55) by educational attainment [HIGH5]   87
4.3 Percentages of married women ('mothers' aged 36–55) agreeing that 'men should work outside, and women should stay home,' by education and employment status [HIGH5]   87
4.4 Employment status of married women by age-group and education [SSM95]   88
4.5 Percentages of married women (aged 30–59) agreeing that 'men should work outside, and women should stay home,' by age-group, education and employment status [SSM95]   89
4.6 Causal diagrams predicted by pre-existing theories   91
4.7 A causal diagram predicted by the hypothesis of rational choice and cognitive dissonance under the constraint of a segmented labour market   95
4.8 Female high-school students' attitude towards the gendered division of labour and their educational aspirations [HIGH5]   96
4.9 Female high-school students' attitude towards the gendered division of labour and their work/career aspirations [HIGH5]   96

4.10 Percentages of female high-school students desiring to enter university, by work/career aspiration and attitude towards the gendered division of labour [HIGH5] 97
4.11 Female high-school students' responses to the question whether job prospects are important in deciding their own post-secondary life-course and their educational aspirations [Hyogo Prefecture, 1981–1982] 99
4.12 Female high-school students' responses to the question whether marriage is important in deciding their own post-secondary life-course and their educational aspirations [Hyogo Prefecture, 1981–1982] 99
4.13 Percentages of female high-school students desiring to enter a university, by gender ideology and types or levels of high schools or tracks [HIGH5] 101
4.14 A hypothetical causal diagram for relevant variables in the typical life-course for Japanese married women 102
4B.1 Wife's and husband's educational levels and husband's mean income (including tax) 109
5.1 Women's economic activity rate 111
5.2 Korean women's labour-force participation rate by age 112
5.3 The analysed respondents 127
5.4 The analysed unit 128

Tables

1.1	Total fertility rate of major countries	5
1.2	Statistical indices relating to employment in Japan: 1975 and 2005	9
1.3	Proportion of people working 50 or more hours per week by country	12
1.4	Changes in attitudes towards work and leisure in Japan: 1973 and 2003	13
1.5	Comparison of time-use in Sweden, UK and Japan: women and men	15
1.6	Preferred life-course for women: 7-country comparison	17
1.7	Wage gap between females and males: 5-country comparison	21
1.8	Attitudes towards career development: which is preferable, a or b?	25
1.9	Youth attitudes towards gendered division of labour: 5-country comparison	28
1.10	Gender comparison of egalitarian gender-role attitudes by SESRA-S	29
1.11	7-country comparison of awareness of gender equality by field: percentages regarding status of men and women as equal	30
2.1	Descriptive statistics of regularly-employed wives and homemaker wives	48
2.2	OLS regression on wife's psychological distress (NFRJ98)	51
2.3	OLS regression on wife's psychological distress (NFRJ03)	52
4.1	Summary of predictions from pre-existing theories on the associations among the relevant variables	93
4.2	Summary of predictions on associations among relevant variables from theories and observed associations	100
4A.1	Goodness-of-fit tests for hierarchical log-linear models relating the education (E), employment or work status (W), and gender ideology or gender-role attitude (R) of 'mothers' (aged 36–55) [HIGH5]	105
4A.2	Goodness-of-fit tests for hierarchical log-linear models relating the education (E), employment or work status (W), gender ideology or gender-role attitude (R), and age (A) of married women (aged 30–59) [SSM95]	106

4A.3 Goodness-of-fit tests for hierarchical log-linear models relating the educational aspiration (E), aspiration for work/career (W), and gender ideology or gender-role attitude (R) of female high-school students [HIGH5]   106
4B.1 Association between husband's and wife's educational levels   108
5.1 Definitions and measuring methods of variables   128
5.2 Characteristics of respondents   129
5.3 Duration from childbirth to return to the labour market and change in employment status (N = 128, Ratio = 100.0)   130
5.4 Duration of job discontinuation according to demographic and household characteristics (N = 70, Ratio = 100.0)   131
5.5 Duration of job discontinuation according to occupational characteristics (N=70, Ratio=100.0)   132
5.6 Characteristics according to whether returning to the labour market after childbirth   134
5.7 Characteristics according to duration until return   136
5.8 Factors determining married women's return to the labour market: Cox regression analysis   138

Preface
Atsuko Suzuki

This book is the sixth volume in the *Social Stratification and Inequality Series*, published as the fruit of research by the Centre for the Study of Social Stratification and Inequality (CSSI) in the Twenty-first Century COE Program of the Tohoku University Graduate School of Arts and Letters. It brings together the results of studies by the Gender Studies Group of the CSSI Minority Division (comprising an Ethnicity Studies Group and Gender Studies Group). Three of the five contributors, including the editor, are CSSI members from the Gender Studies Group, while the remaining two have participated in research which has included presenting at workshops relating to gender and career held by the CSSI.

While empirical research with career and gender as dual frames of reference has been carried out in the two fields of sociology and social psychology, studies tend to be performed independently in each respective field. This means that full mutual advantage is not taken of the results of such research. The elucidation of complex social phenomena in an objective, multi-faceted, systematic manner, however, calls for an interdisciplinary approach. The Gender Studies Group of the CSSI Minority Division has thus continued interdisciplinary research incorporating sociological and social psychological approaches. It has been conducive to a more realistic awareness, understanding and resolution of problems in a variety of issues relating to career and gender. The Gender Studies Group has confirmed the fact that collaboration between these two approaches can make a considerable, mutually-complementary contribution towards these endeavours. This volume is one which brings together the products of that research, and offers suggestions for concrete solutions.

'Gender' is an indicator, or attribute, which culturally or socially characterises a person as female or male. In concrete terms, it means the expected way of being—the personality, role, manner of behaving, way of life, and so on—deemed appropriate to men and women, respectively. Gender is determined by culture, and fulfils a function as a system which continually reproduces the differences between men and women in society through individual behaviour. Gender is not immutable, however, as it changes along with the times and social situation, even within the same culture.

Japanese society traditionally has been taken to be a strongly genderised society with strict gender norms, in which the gendered division of labour stipulated that men should be the breadwinners, while women's place was in the home. It is now in the process of changing its profile. According to longitudinal studies of Japanese attitudes and behaviour since the 1970s, the greatest among the various changes has been that in attitudes and behaviour connected with gender. Specifically, there has been a rapid acceleration in trends towards remaining unmarried, delaying marriage, and declining fertility. Moreover, due in no small part to the impact of the increasingly advanced information-based nature of Japanese society, its globalisation and economic changes, there has also been enormous change relating to career development. While the lifetime employment system is weakening, on the one hand, achievementism and meritism have become pervasive. There is now a marked tendency among young people towards non-regular employment and an increase in job-leaving and job-changing.

The primary aim of this volume is to clarify the mutual inter-relationship between the macro and micro dimensions of society and the individual in an age of great change, through collaboration in empirical research in sociology and social psychology relating to career and gender. More specifically, it seeks to explain, by using Japan as the target of analysis, how changes in individuals' attitudes and behaviour relating to career and gender are connected with the social system, family system, laws, customs, norms, corporate climate, and the like.

The second aim is to deepen readers' understanding of Japan by highlighting the characteristic traits and universals in Japanese society, Japanese culture, the Japanese family, and Japanese people, in terms of gender and career. Analysis and explanation of the nature of career and gender among the Japanese from a sociological and social psychological viewpoint can become useful indicators for grasping the substance of changes in Japanese society and predicting their future direction. The book also compares the nature of career and gender in Japan with that of South Korea, a country which has cultural commonality, from the perspective not only of sociology and social psychology, but also of economics (the labour market), in order to clarify even more sharply the specificity and universality of Japanese society.

The third aim is to banish career- and gender-related social disadvantage and unfairness, and to pursue measures to resolve the universal question of how to achieve autonomous choice, peace of mind and happiness in the home, the workplace and society for the individual.

This book is unique in its employment throughout all but one of its chapters of an interdisciplinary sociological and social psychological approach in dealing with issues of career and gender, with Chapter Five taking an economic approach. An outline of the various chapters now follows.

Chapter One, by Atsuko Suzuki, gives a sociological and social psychological overview of the changes that have occurred in recent years in Japanese people's behaviour and attitudes concerning career and gender, and their determinants, interspersed with cross-cultural comparative data. The overview is expected to prompt readers to deepen their understanding of Japanese society and the Japanese. Further, it elucidates the disincentives towards achievement of a work/life balance in Japan, and, on that basis, explores ways of facilitating autonomous individual career development.

Chapter Two, by Akihide Inaba, uses large-scale, repeated cross-sectional research data to analyse the mental health of wives in permanent jobs who have children aged six or under, and examines the conditions which enable wives in regular employment to juggle their work and family roles, namely, the conditions necessary for the establishment of a work/life balance. The results make it clear that husbands' participation in child-rearing, and husbands' having the opportunity to take nursing leave when their children are sick, et cetera, comprise a vital factor which exerts a positive influence upon the state of mental health of wives in regular employment.

Chapter Three, by Kiriko Sakata, takes up the determinant factors in leadership effectiveness, in order to examine the difficulties which women in managerial positions face in Japan. The chapter minutely analyses the relevant literature in sociology and social psychology. It identifies the organisational factors and individual factors which give rise to gender differences in effectiveness, and elucidates the process by which these factors impact upon the interpersonal interaction between leaders and followers to create such differences. The chapter further advocates a hypothetical model in which individual factors and organisational factors mutually interact to influence followers' processes of interpersonal cognition and mutual interaction vis-à-vis leaders.

Chapter Four, by Kunihiro Kimura, proposes a new hypothetical model of rational choice and cognitive dissonance under the constraint of the segmented labour market. Data are used from a Japanese national Social Stratification and Social Mobility (SSM) survey for the analysis and verification from various angles of what the author terms 'the paradoxical associations among educational attainment, employment status and gender ideology.' The paradox is that highly-educated, married Japanese women lack a proactive attitude towards employment—a high proportion of them being homemaker wives—yet are critical of the gendered division of labour. Further, the chapter empirically confirms the validity of the new model by utilising data from a survey of social consciousness targeting high school students and their parents.

Chapter Five, by Jikyung Kim, uses data from the Korea Labor and Income Panel Study (KLIPS) to analyse determinant factors relating to young, married Korean women's return to the labour market after child-raising, they having quit their jobs upon the birth of their first child. The chapter illustrates the persistent difficulty experienced by married women in obtaining employment, the comparatively long period they spend caring for a first child, and the inverse proportion between women's level of education and the length of career interruption between quitting a job and re-entering the workforce. The results indicate the need for vocational training to facilitate the return to work of women who left employment for childbirth and child-raising, and the importance of corporate motherhood-protection measures and governmental policies to provide assistance with child-rearing expenses.

It is hoped that this volume can contribute not only to the elucidation of universal issues associated with career and gender, but also to the enhancement of interest from outside Japan in Japanese career and gender research, as well as to the promotion of a scholarly exchange of ideas.

Atsuko Suzuki, Editor
June 2007

Acknowledgements

The publication of this volume was made possible by a grant offered by the Centre for the Study of Social Stratification and Inequality (CSSI) in the Twenty-first Century COE Program of the Tohoku University Graduate School of Arts and Letters, whose financial support is gratefully acknowledged. Thanks are due to Airin Izumi, Hiroshi Endō and Hiroaki Ozaki for their excellent administrative work and careful consideration. I would also like to express my special appreciation to one of the contributors, Kunihiro Kimura, for his valuable advice and assistance during the planning stages of this volume. Finally, representing the five contributors, I extend our deepest and genuine gratitude to Dr Leonie Stickland for her excellent translation and Professor Yoshio Sugimoto of La Trobe University, Director of Trans Pacific Press, for his informed advice and patient support throughout the project.

Atsuko Suzuki
June 2007

List of Contributors

Atsuko Suzuki
Professor, Department of Linguistic Science, Graduate School of Arts and Letters, Tohoku University (Social Psychology, Industrial and Organizational Psychology)

Akihide Inaba
Associate Professor, Department of Sociology, Tokyo Metropolitan University (Family Sociology, Social Statistics)

Kiriko Sakata
Associate Professor, Department of Human Sciences, Graduate School of Integrated Arts and Sciences, Hiroshima University (Social Psychology, Group Dynamics)

Kunihiro Kimura
Associate Professor, Department of Behavioral Science, Graduate School of Arts and Letters, Tohoku University (Mathematical/ Quantitative Sociology, Social Psychology)

Jikyung Kim
Associate Research Fellow, National Pension Research Institute, Korea (Home and Consumer Economics)

1 Introduction: Micro–Macro Dynamics

Atsuko Suzuki

As an introduction to the following chapters, Chapter One provides a sociological and social psychological overview of the recent changes in Japanese people's attitudes and behaviour relating to career and gender, punctuated with cross-cultural comparative data. The aim of this outline is to elucidate the dynamic mutual interrelatedness between society and individuals on macro and micro levels. In concrete terms, I will first clarify from a macro perspective what constitutes the changes that have occurred in the past three to four decades in the image of the Japanese family and the Japanese worker, and indicate the existence of various gender issues which hinder career development for both men and women. Next, from a micro perspective, I will consider the change in people's attitudes toward career and gender. Through analysis of these issues, I hope to shed light upon the interrelationship between Japanese society and the attitudes and behaviour of Japanese people.

Career and gender

Work careers and life careers

The term 'career' refers to a person's chain of personal-history events, activities and experiences. Individuals autonomously establish their careers on the basis of their own decisions. Psychology interprets a career as something that grows and develops. The process in which an individual builds his or her career is called 'career development.' Career development has a deep connection with identity, self-concept, individuality and self-image, and subjectively it means the ongoing actualisation of the lifelong development task known as self-realisation (Kanai 2003).

Careers can be roughly categorised as work careers or life careers. A work career is the series of work-related personal-history events, activities, experiences which an individual builds up throughout life. Development of a work career means occupational development in terms of activities, roles, personality, aptitude, interests, abilities, and so on. A life career, on the other hand, is a more comprehensive notion that takes the perspective of lifelong development. Its meaning encompasses the overall evolution of an individual's way of living throughout her or his entire life, including family life, education, hobbies, leisure activities, volunteering and local community activities, as well as the person's work career (Suzuki 2006a). A life career does not recognise value solely in the taking up of an occupation. Instead, it appreciates the individual as a total being, including his or her private life, with emphasis upon autonomous living with the aim of self-realisation in a maturation process as a person. In this chapter, 'career' is understood in this latter sense of a life career.

Life-course choice and gender

The question of the kind of career individuals establish is closely connected with their life-course choice. A life-course is something that traces the changes in role, status, et cetera, at various points in a person's lifetime. A life-course is formed by mutual interaction of social factors—such as the ideology and social system, customs and value system of the times—with factors pertaining to the individual. Specifically speaking, life-course choice means choice involving marriage, family, education and work career. It is thus greatly influenced not only by each individual's gender-role attitudes, but also by the gender norms of the society to which the individual belongs. As there is inequality between the sexes in a heavily-genderised society such as Japan's, where gender norms are strict, and the gendered division of labour stipulates that 'men's place is in the workplace, while women's place is in the home,' there is an even higher likelihood of women and men having divergent career-development processes.

The quest for a work/life balance

As I will later discuss, recent years in Japan have seen an increase in family-orientation among men, while, on the other hand, career-mindedness among women has also risen. In other words, the attitudes of men and women, formerly biased towards work or family, respectively, are changing in the direction of seeking a work/life balance, and the disparity between men and women is shrinking. This tendency is particularly salient among young people. In reality, however, the social situation makes it difficult for both women and men freely to choose a life-course that allows them successfully to juggle work career and family. As well as such social customs, there are inadequacies in the social system, labour policies, and enterprise assistance and childcare services that variously support men and women who continue work while juggling home and workplace. Public expenditure is also meagre. Systemic change in flexible response to changes in people's attitudes is yet to be accomplished. For those reasons, it is not possible to forge a direct link between changes in individuals' attitude vis-à-vis marriage, family and work-career choice, and changes in behaviour according to the substance of the former. The gap between attitude and the social situation has hastened a rapid trend towards later marriage and a declining birth-rate, becoming a factor conducive to great social change.

The changing image of the family

The family exerts a strong influence upon an individual's career development, life-course choice and gender-role attitude, while these factors, in turn, have a huge impact upon the shape of the family. From the latter half of the twentieth century into the present century, the Japanese image of the family has undergone drastic changes, as I indicate below. This transformation is still in progress.

The shift from blood-relationships towards family identity

From the second half of the 1970s into the 1980s, following the end of a period of rapid economic growth, the values courted by Japanese society changed from the satisfaction of material desires to spiritual fulfilment. Around this time, the Japanese family began to shift the focus of its role away from being a place for raising children based on blood-relationships to being a place of mental and physical health, peace of mind and restfulness, based on a subjective awareness—the family identity of its constituent members. It has thus become already impossible to discuss the family solely in terms of a highly-cohesive, exclusive small group composed of close blood-relatives. This demonstrates the extent to which the individualisation and diversification of the family has advanced.

Life-cycle changes due to increasing longevity

In the period from 1970 to 2004, the average life expectancy (the average number of years a newborn child could be expected to live) of Japanese females lengthened from 74.7 to 85.6 years, while that of males increased from 69.3 to 78.6 years (Kōsei Rōdōshō Koyō Kintō/Jidō Katei-kyoku 2004). In the 1940s, the average life expectancy for both males and females was fifty-something, meaning that they did not live very long after the birth of their last child, so there was little necessity to think about how people would spend their remaining years. Now, however, people have as many as thirty or forty years left to live after raising their children. This change in life-cycle is having a great impact upon women's and men's attitudes and behaviour relating to marriage, family and career-development. As family members, it is insufficient for women to fulfil the role exclusively of wife and mother, and for men alone to play the part of breadwinner. It has become necessary for people to aim for life-fulfilment as individuals, and to think about their life-course, reason for living, and self-realisation.

Trends towards later marriage and non-marriage

Until quite recently, Japan was a 'full-marriage society' with an exceptionally high marriage rate. Even today, a little fewer than ninety per cent of never-married people have a desire to marry (Kokuritsu Shakai Hoshō/Jinkō Mondai Kenkyūjo 2006). In spite of this, there is a rapidly-escalating tendency for Japanese to marry late, or not at all. The age at first marriage in 1970 was 24.2 years for wives and 26.9 for husbands. It has continued to rise from then on, reaching 28.0 and 29.8 years, respectively, in 2005 (Kōsei Rōdōshō 2006). Since 1990, the lifetime-unmarried rate (the proportion of the population never having married by the age of fifty) for males has overtaken that of females, the rates in 2000 being 5.8 per cent for women and 12.6 per cent for men (Kokuritsu Shakai Hoshō/Jinkō Mondai Kenkyūjo 2005).

The causes for these later-marriage and non-marriage trends are multiple (Suzuki 2007). One could cite such reasons as the popularisation of higher education for women and their heightened inclination towards continued employment; the destabilisation of employment among young people due to an increase in non-regular employees such as casuals or 'freeters' (the latter being a Japanese neologism combining the words 'free' and '*Arbeiter*' (German for 'worker'), meaning young, unstable workers who neither continue their education nor obtain regular employment after graduating from school); or the reduced necessity for marriage due to heightened freedom in sexual behaviour and the commercialisation and externalisation of domestic labour, thanks to convenience stores and suchlike. In psychological terms, the view that the economic obligations and the responsibilities for the protection and raising of children which marriage entails are too heavy a burden, or that they rob people of behavioural or temporal freedom, also becomes a factor contributing to the avoidance or postponement of marriage.

Declining fertility

In 2005, Japan became the society with the world's lowest birth-rate and ageing population (Sōmushō 2006), and also entered an age of declining population. Its total fertility rate (TFR) dropped from 4.50 in 1950 to 2.00 in 1975, reaching 1.25 in 2005. This figure was second only to South Korea's, which recorded the world's lowest TFR of 1.08 in 2005 (see Table 1.1). Moreover, not only did Japan's trend towards later marriages escalate, but mothers' age at the birth of their first child hit 29.1 years, more than three years higher than the 25.7 years of 1975 (Kōsei Rōdōshō 2006). Declining fertility will cause a labour shortage in Japan in the near future. As I state below, a series of laws has been enacted and progressive adjustments in the employment environment made with the aim of providing equal opportunity for employment and support for a balance between work and family, in order actively to promote women's advance into society and to make full use of their abilities.

It is difficult clearly to specify the cause of the declining birth-rate, but factors common to developed countries, including the soaring expense of child-rearing, are presumed to figure largely. The increase in non-regular employees due to economic stagnation since the 1990s

Table 1.1: Total fertility rate of major countries

Country	Total fertility rate	Year
United States	2.07	2003
France	1.90	2004
Sweden	1.75	2005
United Kingdom	1.74	2004
Germany	1.37	2004
Italy	1.33	2004
Japan	1.25	2005
Korea	1.08	2005

Source: Compiled from Nihon Keizai Shimbun 2006.

has worsened the economic situation of young people and inflated their anxiety about the future—another factor of great influence. Another conceivable reason for the fall in the birth-rate could be that the higher women's average age is at first marriage, the higher their age of commencement of child-bearing will be, thus making stricter demands upon them in terms of stamina. In practice, Japanese women begin to avoid child-bearing once they reach their late thirties. Additional factors which could be cited as characteristic of Japan are its strong social norms which place importance on the legitimacy of children, and the extremely small proportion of children born outside marriage (illegitimate children) in comparison to other developed countries, Japan having less than two per cent illegitimacy (Sweden 55.4 per cent, United Kingdom 42.3 per cent, and Italy 14.9 per cent in 2004) (Eurostat 2005). On the other hand, though, births from so-called '*dekichatta kekkon* (shotgun marriages)' (marriages triggered by unplanned pregnancy) accounted for 26.7 per cent of firstborn babies (Kōsei Rōdōshō 2006). As well as these personal reasons, the fact that there are not enough public child-care facilities which would provide prolonged care for children probably constitutes another cause. Moreover, the number of obstetricians and obstetric clinics has plummeted dramatically in recent times, and this has raised the hurdles against child-bearing even higher.

If one analyses the decline in fertility from a psychological perspective, one could attribute it to a loss of unequivocalness in the value of children (Kashiwagi 2006). The attitude among women in their twenties and thirties that they need not have children is especially marked. The economic merit of having children has shrunk, as children no longer comprise a labour force, and parents are also less likely to count on their sons looking after them in their old age. Children have become a source of pleasure, joy and encouragement in their parents' lives, and there are increasing numbers of parents who, having come to expect their children to be their partners in conversation or to assume the role of carers when they grow old, want daughters more than sons.

An ageing population

Concomitant with the progressive decline in the birth-rate, the ageing of the Japanese population is also rapidly accelerating, its proportion of people under fifteen years of age hitting a world low of 13.6 per cent in 2005, while people aged sixty-five or over accounted for 21.0

per cent of the total population. Japan outstripped Italy and Germany to become the world's most ageing society (Sōmushō 2006). This distortion in the age-structure, weighted towards older people, has spawned concern that it will trigger problems in Japanese society on a variety of fronts, including pensions, employment and health-care issues.

Trends towards smaller families and single-person households

The average number of members in a household has shrunk greatly, from 3.35 people in 1975 to 2.60 in 2005 (Sōmushō 2006). The proportion of single-person households also increased from 18.2 per cent in 1975 to 23.3 per cent in 2003 (Kōsei Rōdōshō 2003). Three-generation families living under the one roof became fewer, while there was an increase in households composed of just a married couple and those where an elderly person aged sixty-five or older lived alone.

The changing image of the worker

Changes in the work behaviour of Japanese women

Here, based upon the work of Suzuki (2006a), I will elucidate the changes that have occurred since the 1960s in Japanese women's attitudes and behaviour vis-à-vis work, in comparison with those of men.

Up to the mid-1970s

Until the 1960s in Japan, it was the norm for women to labour as family workers in independent businesses or in agriculture, forestry or fisheries, and so on, or as employees in blue-collar occupations. From that point on, however, against a backdrop of changes in industrial structure due to rapid economic growth (the decline of primary industry and the flourishing of tertiary industry), the rapid lengthening of the average life expectancy, the inflow of population to cities, a proliferation in employees and a shortage of labour power, there was an increase in women hired to do white-collar work outside the home in clerical jobs or occupations requiring specialised expertise. At the same time, though, from the 1960s into the 1970s, the stay-at-home housewife in the nuclear family became the target of the aspirations of many young women, as a symbol of an affluent lifestyle. There was progressive 'housewifisation (Hara and Seiyama 2005),' in which the proportion of women who quit their jobs after having worked only for a short period because of marriage and thereafter devoted themselves to housework overtook that of the previous generation. The labour-force participation rate for young women continued to fall until the mid-1970s (Hara and Seiyama 2005). At that time, gender roles had controlling values in both the home and the workplace. Women working under a social and economic system based on these values were seldom treated as independent professionals equal to men. Not treating women equally to men as professionals was justified on the grounds that women had the role of wife and mother, and that they should have the personality, occupation and way of life befitting that role. By the same token, it was seen as natural for fathers, being professional workers, to be exempted from their roles and responsibilities in the home, and to be absent from it.

From the mid-1970s to the 1980s
After the mid-1970s, however, especially around the tail-end of Japan's period of rapid economic growth, this 'housewifisation' halted, the labour-force participation rate of young women turned upwards, and part-timisation began to advance (Hara and Seiyama 2005). There was also a decrease in lifetime never-employed females, and there was a marked increase in the proportion of women who entered employment after finishing their schooling (Yamaguchi 1998). In 1975, the proportion of married women among female employees (excluding widows and divorcees) overtook that of the unmarried, coming to constitute the majority, and since then, married women continued to maintain their share in the high fiftieth percentile till 2005 (see Table 1.2). Conversely, the proportion of married women who were homemaker wives in white-collar 'salaryman' households, which peaked at 37.1 per cent in 1980, has continued to decline, reaching 26.5 per cent in 2000 (Naikakufu 2002).

From the latter half of the 1970s through into the 1980s, men's role as family breadwinner was still taken for granted. But the importance of the role of the father began to be acknowledged in the context of the above-mentioned changes in women. Moreover, attitudinal change reflecting the values of gender equality, individualism, respect for human rights and the like, as part of the maturation of democracy, emerged among the Japanese. Under such influences as the United Nations Decade for Women (1976–1985), the ratification by Japan of the Convention on the Elimination of All Forms of Discrimination

Table 1.2: Statistical indices relating to employment in Japan: 1975 and 2005

Indices	1975 Females	1975 Males	2005 Females	2005 Males
1. Ratio of employed females with spouse	51.3%	–	56.8%	–
2. Ratio of females among employed persons	32.0%	–	41.3%	–
3. Ratio of short-time workers among the employed	17.4%	6.4%	40.6%	12.4%
4. Ratio of females among the short-time employed	56.4%	–	69.7%	–
5. Ratio of university & graduate-school graduates among female workers	2.9%[a]	–	17.2%	–
6. Ratio of females among corporate officials	3.1%[a]	–	10.4%	–
7. Mean years per worker of continuous work[b]	5.3 yrs	9.8 yrs	8.7 yrs	13.4 yrs

Notes: Short-time employees: non-agricultural, non-forestry employees working less than 35 hours per week. Corporate officials: division head, section head, sub-section head. a = 1980. b = excluding short-time workers.
Source: Compiled from Kōsei Rōdōshō Koyō Kintō/Jidō Katei-kyoku (ed.) 2006.

against Women (1985), and the enactment of the Equal Employment Opportunity Law (1985) which prohibits discrimination against women, people's attitudes relating to the roles of men and women in society have diversified.

Since the 1990s

After the start of the 1990s, various laws were enacted with the aim of promoting sexual equality in the workplace and enabling a balance between workplace and home for both women and men: the Child-care Leave Law (1991); the Revised Equal Employment Opportunity Law (1999); the Basic Law for a Gender-Equal Society (1999); the Child-care and Family-care Leave Law (2005); and the Law for Measures to Support the Development of the Next Generation (2005); and there was progressive improvement in employment-related legislation for enterprises and local government bodies. There were more women continuing work even after marriage and childbirth, and family-mindedness among men grew stronger. Women's share of the total workforce had grown almost continuously since 1960, to reach 41.3 per cent in 2005 (see Table 1.2). This increase in the female share is called the 'feminisation of employment.' The proportion of female regular employees consisting of women with high educational qualifications has also risen, and there has been a gradual increase in female executives in recent years (see Table 1.2). Within this growth in female employees, though, there has been more hiring of non-regular workers such as part-timers and contracted or temporary staff than of regular employees, and females account for around seventy per cent of short-time workers (see Table 1.2). With the addition of freelancers and teleworkers, diversification in the forms of women's non-regular employment is advancing. In the case of males, also, there is an increase in so-called 'NEETs (Not in Education, Employment or Training)' and non-regular workers, especially among the young. From a macro perspective, the Japanese labour market is undergoing progressive polarisation into regular- and non-regular employment, the widening income gap between the two poles now becoming a serious social problem.

The current state of Japanese work from a gender perspective

If one interprets Japanese society on a macro level, gender is stratified, and the strata are expressed in terms of gender, because of men's advantage over women due to the gendered division of labour (Hashimoto 1999). This division of labour along gender lines tenaciously exists not only in the individual psyche, but also in families, enterprises and society, and there is a continuation of practices in line with it. The gendered division of labour has been reproduced and maintained amid these practices. Even now, in the twenty-first century, there continues a vicious cycle in which practices connected with the gendered labour division in enterprises, in particular, have reinforced the division of labour in the home, and the gendered division of labour in the home has made the gendered labour division in the business world into an impregnable system (Suzuki 2006a). As a result, many women have laboured in workplaces where the three factors of short length of service, an auxiliary position and low remuneration have operated in unison (Kumazawa 2000).

While marriage and childbirth accounted for 25.2 per cent of the reasons for women quitting work in 1975, these had dropped to 8.2 per cent in 2004 (Kōsei Rōdōshō Koyō Kintō/Jidō Katei-kyoku 2006). Though there are more women continuing paid work even after giving birth, there are still many women who have quit their jobs in spite of a desire to stay at work, because conditions were not in place to enable them to keep working upon marriage or childbirth. This fact again illustrates that there are still insufficient arrangements in the working environment aimed at a work/life balance.

As previously stated, though there has been a certain amount of progress in legislative improvements such as would make it easier for married women to continue working, the social system, workplace organisation, workplace climate, and workplace support and services do not constitute a framework commensurate with these legal developments. There are contradictions between the laws and various systems. Examples of the latter that have been set up include the care insurance system, under which the elderly will not receive sufficient care unless families also look after them because the system alone is inadequate, and the system of taxation, pensions and wages which is more advantageous to homemaker wives than to working wives. Because these systems are modelled upon a 'standard household' (husband, homemaker wife and two children) where the gendered division of labour in the home is established, it is of greater advantage to married women to work merely to supplement the household budget rather than to work in a financially independent manner. For that reason, from before World War II through to the present day, the work of married women in Japan has often been for the sake of supplementing household finances. In other words, it has been non-regular employment for such purposes as children's educational expenses or housing loan repayments, and, moreover, women have stayed in jobs for a shorter period than men (see Table 1.2). This has made women come to fulfil the function of an economic control-valve. In addition, women who are able to work similarly long hours to men can become regular employees, but women who cannot work such hours are in a position where they have no alternative but to take jobs as non-regular employees.

The flawed work environment in Japanese society is a problem not solely for women, because men, too, pay a high price. Stratification and inequality exist among men, as well, stemming from such factors as educational background, status, income and mode of employment. Moreover, due to the impact of protracted economic stagnation from the 1990s, there was an increase in corporate restructuring, a decline in the recruitment of regular employees, and a rise in the youth unemployment rate, accompanied simultaneously by an increase in non-regular employees such as casuals and freeters. What is more, young people's attitudes towards careers and support for lifetime

Table 1.3: *Proportion of people working 50 or more hours per week by country (%)*

Japan	28.1
New Zealand	21.3
United States; Australia	20.0
United Kingdom	15.5
Greece; Ireland	6.2
France	5.7
Germany; Portugal	5.3
Finland	4.5
Italy	4.2
Belgium	3.8
Austria	2.7
Sweden	1.9
Netherlands	1.4

Source: Compiled from Nihon Keizai Shimbun 2004b.
Data: ILO (as of 2000).

employment and the work ethic weakened, while the attrition rate and labour turnover escalated. As a consequence of these changes, overtime work increased as the number of regular employees fell, and working hours became extremely long (see Table 1.3). This has worsened the work environment for men and provoked an increase in the number of workers with mental health problems due to stress and overwork, including depression and suicide.

Moreover, there still remains a deep-seated value which defines a loyal company employee as one who puts in long hours at work. In recent years, though, there has been an increase in men who do wish to balance their work and home lives (Sōrifu 2000). There are growing numbers, especially among young men, who regard a desirable way of living as one in which priority is given to the balance between work and private life, including time spent with friends and family, time for study, and leisure time (see Table 1.4). In reality, however, most males likely to be socially dominant over females are also constricted by job-centred values such as those epitomised by a large amount of overtime and long hours of work, and it is hard to say that they have autonomously established an affluent life career while prioritising their private life (Suzuki 2006a). As I have previously stated, given the environmental factors in Japanese society, the situation makes

Table 1.4: Changes in attitudes towards work and leisure in Japan: 1973 and 2003 (%)

	Work-oriented	Work/leisure-balance-oriented	Leisure-oriented
1973			
Men	54	19	25
Women	35	23	38
2003			
Men	30	38	30
Women	21	37	38
Young men	22	49	28
Young women	15	51	32

Notes: Targets of survey: aged 16–59. Young: aged 16–29. Leisure: deepening one's connection with friends and family; doing what one enjoys; resting; exercise; social activities; acquiring knowledge.

Source: Compiled from NHK Hōsō Bunka Kenkyūjo 2004.

it difficult for both women and men to juggle private life and work purely through individual effort. This has become a trigger factor in the trend towards remaining single, having fewer children, and the increase in NEETs, freeters and non-regular employees among male and female youth (Suzuki 2006b).

In terms of its social environment relating to declining fertility and gender-equality issues (public policy, the social/economic system and the values which govern behaviour), Japan recorded the lowest rise in the female labour-force participation rate over the past three decades among twenty-four member countries of the Organisation for Economic Co-operation and Development (OECD) with a GDP greater than US$10,000 per head of population (year 2000). It also failed to reach the mean value in any field (the capacity for work/life balance; the degree of adequacy of support in child-rearing; the flexibility of role-sharing in the home; the level of acceptance of diversity in society; the degree of equality in employment opportunity; and so on), with the exception of societal safety and degree of reassurance (Naikakufu Danjo Kyōdō Sankaku Kaigi 2005). Japanese corporate efforts towards the realisation of a work/life balance have only just begun, and have not yet reached the stage of fruition. The Revised Equal Employment Opportunity Law prohibiting gender discrimination and indirect discrimination against men and women will only come into effect from April 2007.

Gender issues impeding career development

Below, I will variously introduce and explore the principal concrete factors which, in combination, impede the kind of career development simultaneously enabling the achievement of a work/life balance. These are problems concerning not only female workers, but their male counterparts, as well.

Family factors

The psychological impact of multiple roles

Working women and men assume multiple roles: family roles and work roles. The psychological impact of multiple roles is considered to be greater for women, as their family responsibilities are heavier than men's due to gender norms, and multiple roles have been treated mainly as a role-conflict issue for women. There is a growing tendency for women not to marry or bear children in order to avoid this conflict, and the trend towards non-marriage and having fewer children is escalating. At present, moreover, the employment of married women is increasing while the family-mindedness of men is on the rise, and there is a gradual increase in male participation in housework and child-care. Growing numbers of men, however, are also experiencing role-conflict because they cannot sufficiently perform their family role, due partly to the influence of long working hours. Because of their excessive working hours, men fall easy prey to physical or mental health problems, and the more value husbands place upon their family role, the greater their multiple-role conflict becomes. In addition, as the further decline in fertility and the ageing of the population will lead to women and men taking on the role of carers for their parents in future, there is likely to be a growing need to consider the psychological impact of this.

Multiple roles give rise to a complex psychological structure by exerting positive influences (encouragement; vitality) and negative influences (overwork; tension). Multiple roles are linked with levels of job satisfaction, organisational commitment, feelings of happiness, family satisfaction, life satisfaction, marital satisfaction and mental health (physical responses to stress, psychological distress/depression, anxiety, et cetera). In dual-income couples, the woman has higher work-family conflict and negative spill-over from her family role to her work role. Even while finding their work role worthwhile, women are thought to have a strong sense of responsibility for their family role, choosing to discontinue employment or to work short hours in order to circumvent the negative influence of their multiple roles. Nevertheless, there remains a deep-rooted awareness in both males and females that men give priority to their work.

The lightness of men's domestic work obligations

Men do indeed prioritise their work. Consequently, their burden relating to domestic chores and their children's education is extremely small. In recent years, the ratio of husbands who share such unpaid work as preparing meals or clearing up afterwards has risen, but there is a large gender gap in the time-allocation of Japanese married couples when compared with other countries. Role-sharing is far from gender-equal. The average time spent per day on domestic work is three hours and one minute for women, but only seventeen minutes for men (see Table 1.5). Even in couples where both spouses are employed, the husband's time spent on domestic work does not increase. The proportion of domestic work performed by all members of the family, including children, is also small (Naikakufu Danjo

Table 1.5: *Comparison of time-use in Sweden, UK and Japan: women and men*

	Sweden		United Kingdom		Japan	
	W	M	W	M	W	M
Free time	5.03	5.24	5.05	5.30	5.17	5.46
Food-related	2.28	2.11	2.16	2.04	3.37	2.52
Sleeping	8.11	8.01	8.27	8.18	7.38	7.52
Commuting	1.23	1.30	1.25	1.30	0.22	0.41
Domestic work	3.42	2.29	4.15	2.18	3.01	0.17
Occupation	3.12	4.25	2.33	4.18	3.04	5.39

Notes: W = women; M = men. Units: Hours and minutes. Free time = hobbies, entertainment, television, etc., resting, relaxation, sports, volunteer activities, socialising. Food-related = meals, personal errands, shopping. Commuting = travelling between home and workplace or school/university. Domestic work = household chores, child-care, family-care. Occupation = work, study. Japanese figures do not total 24 hours because such categories as 'Other' were excluded.
European data: Compiled from Eurostat, European Commission 2004, Tables 1.1 and 1.2. Respondents: men and women aged 20–74.
Japanese data: Compiled from Sōmuchō Tōkei-kyoku 2002, Table 1. Respondents: men and women aged 15 and over (including aged 75 and over).
Source: Compiled from Suzuki 2006b, Table 7.7.

Figure 1.1: Parental time spent with children: 6-country comparison

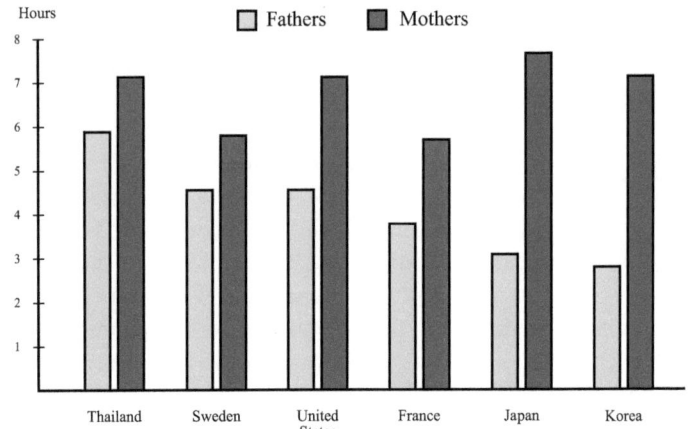

Note: Hours spent on weekdays with children aged 12 or under
Source: Compiled from Kokuritsu Josei Kyōiku Kaikan 2006.

Kyōdō Sankaku-kyoku 2002). The average time fathers spend with their children on weekdays is the second-shortest in the world, after Korea (See Figure 1.1).

Life-course factors

Compared with other countries, Japan has a higher ratio of people who think an appropriate life-course for women is to quit work for childbirth and child-care, then to resume employment (mainly as non-regular employees) after raising their children, in accordance with the values of the gendered division of labour (see Table 1.6). The product of this is the M-shaped labour pattern and the issue of part-time work.

The M-shaped women's labour-force participation rate
Though there has been a reduction in women quitting their jobs because of marriage or childbirth, when questioned about their occupation one and a half years after the birth of their first child, sixty-one per cent of women who had originally been employed answered 'no occupation,' and ninety per cent of those women had left their work before childbirth (Kōsei Rōdōshō 2004). In other words, half of the women who had been working had quit their jobs

Table 1.6: Preferred life-course for women: 7-country comparison (%)

	Unemployed	Until marriage	Until childbirth	Indefinitely	Re-employment
Japan	2.8	4.0	7.0	41.0	40.9
Korea	1.2	1.7	3.5	52.5	38.6
Philippines	6.0	24.5	12.5	41.3	15.0
United States	0.7	0.5	3.5	56.4	18.3
Sweden	0.0	0.0	0.5	77.8	4.0
Germany	0.0	1.9	7.7	55.8	27.1
United Kingdom	0.4	0.7	3.1	51.1	24.6

Notes: Respondents: men and women aged 20–59. Unemployed = women should not be employed. Until marriage = women had better work until marriage. Until childbirth = women had better work until childbirth. Indefinitely = women had better continue working, even if having children. Re-employment = women had better quit work if having children, and return to work after children grow. Totals do not add up to 100 due to exclusion of 'Other' and 'Do not know' responses.

Source: Compiled from Naikakufu Danjo Kyōdō Sankaku-kyoku 2002, Table on p. 66.

before giving birth. The existence of the corporate practices of women quitting work upon childbirth and long hours of overtime work are the principal factors which trigger job termination. As a result of such life-course choices, the labour-force participation rate by age of Japanese women in 2005 traced an M-shape with the late twenties and late forties as the peaks, between which it bottomed out in the thirties: the child-raising age (See Figure 1.2). This M-curve described by the labour-force participation rate by age is characteristic of women's employment in societies with a strong consciousness of the gendered division of labour. In developed countries of the West which originally had a similar tendency to Japan, women's M-curve disappeared after the 1980s, and their labour participation has now assumed a plateau-shape similar to that of men's.

In Japan in recent years, however, there has also been a rise in the labour-force participation rate for women in their late twenties to their early thirties and a gradual departure from this M-curve, due to a heightening in young women's awareness vis-à-vis continued employment and the desire for self-realisation through work, thanks also to the enshrining of child-care leave into law. If women can utilise family networks, child-care centres or babysitters to whom they can confidently entrust their children, then their work-continuation rate is likely to climb further, and the M-curve to disappear.

Figure 1.2: *Transitions in the labour-force participation rate in Japan: 1975 and 2005*

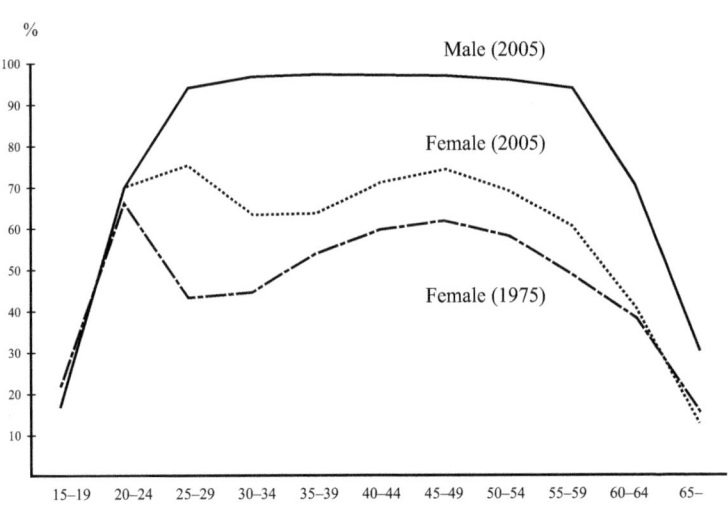

Labour-force participation rate: proportion of the population aged fifteen or over in the labour force
Source: Compiled from Kōsei Rōdōshō Koyō Kintō/Jidō Katei-kyoku 2006, Appendix Table 2.

The difficulty of taking child-care leave

Workers taking child-care leave accounted for 70.6 per cent of all those who gave birth in the 2003 fiscal year, and, in comparison by gender, 96.1 per cent of people who took the leave were females, as opposed to the 3.9 per cent who were males (Kōsei Rōdōshō Koyō Kintō/Jidō Katei-kyoku 2006). The greatest factor hindering men from taking such leave is its unpaid nature. In addition, as corporate attitudes are often not clearly articulated in relation to how the taking of this leave might impact upon the taker's personnel evaluation, men's fears that promotions and pay increases might be delayed are intensified. In actual fact, such delays do often occur. Moreover, the workplace atmosphere and the reaction of superiors are not necessarily conducive to the taking of leave, either. Irrespective of the increasing numbers of young men who desire to participate in child-rearing, flaws in the personnel-evaluation system and ambiguities in its operation have made it difficult for that wish to become reality. Though the Law for Measures to Support the

Development of the Next Generation was enacted in 2005, there have been numerous disadvantages to taking such time off—not only in economic aspects, but also in terms of career development, and this fact has made it especially hard for men to take the leave.

The taking of child-care leave is not problematical solely for those who take it, however, but also for the workplace as a whole. In shorthanded businesses, for example, replacements have to be secured. Nowadays, when non-marriage and delayed marriage are on the rise, it is also not uncommon for a considerable proportion of employees in a workplace to be childless. Measures to support a work/life balance should be prevented from benefiting only people who take child-care leave. There is a call for consideration towards the enhancement of measures such as would enable the attainment of a balance between private life and work from a broader and fairer perspective.

The growth in part-time employment

The proportion of regular employees among female employees (excluding company officers) plummeted from 61.6 per cent (males: 91.5 per cent) in 1994 to 47.5 per cent in 2005 (males: 82.3 per cent) (Kōsei Rōdōshō Koyō Kintō/Jidō Katei-kyoku 2006). By contrast, in the same period, part-timers increased from 28.1 per cent (males: 0.9 per cent) to 32.8 per cent (males: 2.7 per cent) (Kōsei Rōdōshō Koyō Kintō/Jidō Katei-kyoku 2006). Part-timers and temporary employees whose jobs are insecure make up the major part of the increase in the female employed labour pool. In Japan, there is a unique tendency for the ratio of part-timers to increase rather than to decrease along with a rise in the female labour-force participation rate. Many female workers are hired as non-regular employees, and this reproduces the gendered division of labour present in the workplace and the home, respectively.

The motivation for female part-timers to desire non-regular employment in the case of the majority of women aged twenty-four or under is: 'There is nowhere to work that meets my wishes.' Among women aged between thirty and the early forties, the majority says: 'I would have wanted to be a regular employee had I not had to do child-care, housework or family care.' Women with a strong desire for regular employment but who are forced to become part-timers because of external factors account for more than sixty per cent in every age-group apart from that of women in their late twenties who are at child-rearing age.

Part-time work is supposed to mean shorter working hours than a full-time job, but there are many Japanese part-timers who work full-time hours, and so the concept cannot be defined in hourly terms (Miyama 2000). Moreover, though the wage disparity between female regular employees and part-timers had already reached an average of about ninety in comparison to the regular employee standard of 100 in countries of the European Union in the mid-1990s (Miyama 2000), in Japan, it was 69.0 in 2005—the gap having widened from 76.2 in 1980 (Kōsei Rōdōshō Koyō Kintō/Jidō Katei-kyoku 2006). There is also a large disparity between the two types of employment in systems involving not only wages but also child-care leave and working hours. Enterprises that have a system of converting part-timers into regular employees are still a small minority.

The problem of inequity in non-regular employment, including part-time work, was long deemed an issue of concern only to female workers, and its consequent invisibility in social terms meant that its importance was seldom afforded notice. When an increase in corporate restructuring triggered by the post-1990 economic downturn led to a rise in the youth unemployment rate, however, there was simultaneous growth in male non-regular workers. The existence of strata and inequality between men according to mode of employment became evident when, for example, men who were non-regular employees were unable to marry or have children because of insufficient income. As a result, non-regular employment has come to be recognised as a serious social problem in recent years.

Workplace factors

Sex segregation

Japanese corporate organisations are markedly genderised, and so-called sex segregation, in which women's and men's occupations and types of work differ in terms of content and scale, is well-advanced. Not only does the corporate side treat men and women differently, being mired in the norms of the gendered division of labour, but women themselves also have occasion voluntarily to choose that division. The types of work and occupations where women tend to congregate, constituting so-called 'pink-collar jobs' which are supposedly 'suited to females,' tend to have low status and prestige, and there are also few opportunities for promotion or advancement in rank. Other examples of segregation are the high ratio of females among part-timers and temporary employees, and the 'routine clerical track' (in which more than ninety per cent of workers are women) within the track-differentiated labour management system. Even in occupations in high-level professional and managerial categories, women and men are frequently separated according to a hierarchy of prestige in specialist fields. Segregation by sex has become a hotbed of indirect discrimination against women.

The scale of the gendered wage disparity

Sex segregation provokes a wage gap between males and females. The principal reason for women feeling dissatisfied in the workplace or wanting to change jobs, irrespective of age, is low wages (Kōsei Rōdōshō Koyō Kintō/Jidō Katei-kyoku 2005). This dissatisfaction is one of the main contributing factors that promote women's leaving work or switching jobs, and prompt them to return to the home. The wage disparity between females and males in Japan is large in comparison with other countries (see Table 1.7). In recent years, the gap has been closing, but, generally, many women are non-regular employees. Even if women *are* regular employees, their years of continuous employment are comparatively few (see Table 1.2). They seldom enjoy the benefits of lifetime employment or a seniority-based wage system. Women are also the underdogs in such aspects as job classification, education and training, promotion and personnel transfer. Furthermore, in regard to the family benefits and housing allowances which are paid to heads of households, because men comprise the majority of householders, not many women accordingly receive such payments. As a result, women's pay is less than men's. Even where men and women do the same job under the same employer, there are subtle differences in their responsibilities and job content, and the principle of comparable worth is not observed. The wage differential between females and males, and between regular and non-regular employees, is also part

Table 1.7: Wage gap between females and males: 5-country comparison

Country	Wage gap	Year
Australia	86.4	2004
Netherlands	80.5	2004
United Kingdom	76.8	2004
Japan	65.9	2005
Korea	63.9	2002

Note: Male wage = 100

Source: Compiled from Kōsei Rōdōshō Koyō Kintō/Jidō Katei-kyoku 2006, Appendix Table 101.

of the reason for the perpetuation of the gendered division of labour in the home.

The low percentage of female executives
The proportion of females among personnel in managerial positions in Japan is extremely low in comparison with other countries (see Figure 1.3). Women's share of executive positions in private enterprise is increasing slightly, but as the job classification becomes higher, the proportion of women falls. Firms which had voluntarily introduced positive (affirmative) action by the 2003 fiscal year in order to make optimum use of women amounted to roughly thirty per cent of all businesses—the larger the firm, the higher being its rate of adoption of positive action (Kōsei Rōdōshō Koyō Kintō/Jidō Katei-kyoku 2006).

The difficulty of re-employment and low fluidity of the labour market
In a similar manner to Korea and the countries of southern Europe, Japan comprises a 'rigid society' where it is difficult for people to be re-hired once they leave their jobs. A prominent characteristic of career development among Japanese employees is the advantageousness of

Figure 1.3: Ratio of women among employees in managerial positions: 8-country comparison

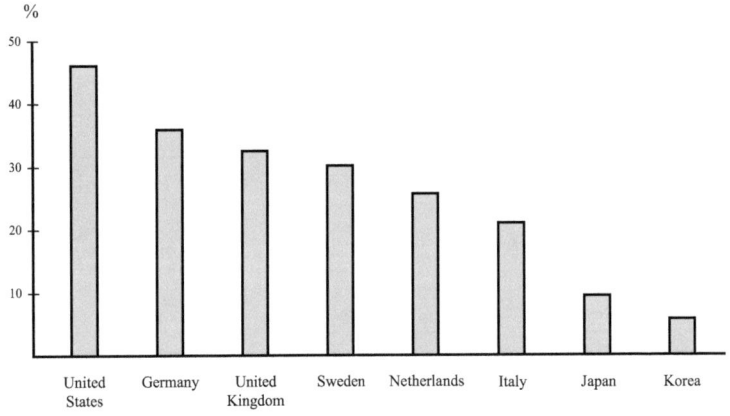

United States, Netherlands: 2002; Japan: 2004; Germany, United Kingdom, Sweden, Italy, Korea: 2003.
Data: ILO 'LABORSTA.'
Source: Compiled from Kōsei Rōdōshō Koyō Kintō/Jidō Katei-kyoku 2005, Appendix Tables 13 and 99.

continuing to work for a lengthy period for the same company, as is illustrated by the lifetime employment system. Quitting a job often leads to disadvantages in terms of pay and promotion. Enterprises are reluctant to introduce a re-employment system, and there are insufficient measures for maintaining and enhancing the occupational capability of workers on child-care leave (Kōsei Rōdōshō 2005). Age restrictions, or a lack of skills, experience or qualifications make it hard for many women to find a workplace that will re-employ them, and the conditions are often worse than in their previous job. This is disadvantageous to women's work career development. The monetary amount involved in terms of opportunity cost, which women lose by quitting regular employment because of childbirth or child-rearing, is exceedingly large. It is necessary for all firms either to expand their re-hiring system, or, through mobility in the labour market as a whole, to ensure that re-entry to the workforce is easy and not economically disadvantageous.

Social factors

The inadequacy of the social system and social policy

The conventional Japanese social system and social policies concerned with work are structured on a foundation of 'enterprises in which male regular employees labour under the ethos of priority to efficiency and self-sacrificing service, and families in which those men are sustained by homemaker wives.' The content of family policy also supports this structure. For example, though it is a married woman's individual free choice whether to become a homemaker wife, the current systems of taxation, pensions and wages are modelled on the 'standard household,' and are thus disadvantageous to dual-income households or to singles. Considering that the ratio of households with a homemaker wife has dropped below that of dual-income households, and there has been a marked increase in single-person households in recent years, there will be a need in the near future to establish a system with the individual, rather than the household, as its basic unit.

The rigidity of child-care services

Child-care services are not responding to the diverse needs of working parents. Examples include an absence of flexibility in the timing of enrolment, a mismatch between facilities' enrolment criteria and working mothers' hours of work or financial situation, and a lack of child-care centres which accept babies aged less than one year, or infants whose parents have just resumed work after child-care leave. Moreover, though the number of women who work at night is increasing—the prohibition on night work for females having been lifted in April 1999—there has not been commensurate growth in night-time child-care facilities properly accredited to look after children until a late hour.

Women's and men's attitudinal change to career and gender

Taking as background my discussion up to this point of Japanese people's behaviour and issues connected with career and gender, I will now clarify the kinds of changes that have occurred in men's and women's attitudes over the past thirty to forty years, mainly by use of social psychological data.

Attitudes towards career development among the highly-educated

Characteristic of the attitudes towards career development among female and male graduates of four-year universities aged in their mid-twenties is the importance both genders place upon the appraisal of ability, self-realisation, and the enrichment of personal life (Suzuki 2004) (see Table 1.8). In other words, they seek assessment of their ability and qualifications rather than an appraisal based on seniority or company loyalty, and want to develop a career based on work which is worth doing, enables full play to be given to their abilities, and which they like. In addition, they give more weight to enrichment of such aspects of private life as family and leisure activities, rather than job fulfilment, as their lifestyle during career development. These characteristics illustrate that the values emphasised in career development have undergone a great transformation in recent years, from work-centred to individual-centred values. At the same time, they also clearly indicate that the gender gap has disappeared from attitudes towards career development in the case of young people with a high educational background.

Support for a work/life-balanced life-course
According to a survey on women's life course, the view that 'women also should work outside the home' is supported by nearly eighty

Table 1.8: Attitudes towards career development: which is preferable, a or b?

Item	Men (77) % (N)	Women (54) % (N)
1. a. Seniority-focused	24.7 (19)[c]	29.6 (16)[d]
b. Merit-payment-focused	75.3 (58)	70.4 (38)
2. a. Appraisal of company spirit, loyalty and character	8.0 (6)[c]	7.5 (4)[c]
b. Appraisal of ability, skills and qualifications	92.2 (71)	92.5 (49)
3. a. Working conditions are good, but work is disliked	15.6 (12)[c]	13.2 (7)[c]
b. Working conditions are not good, but work is liked	84.4 (65)	86.8 (46)
4. a. Pay is high, but work is not rewarding	20.8 (16)[c]	15.4 (8)[c]
b. Pay is low, but work is rewarding	79.2 (61)	84.6 (44)
5. a. Pay is high, but work does not give full play to abilities	27.3 (21)[c]	16.7 (9)[c]
b. Pay is low, but work gives full play to abilities	72.7 (56)	83.3 (45)
6. a. Job fulfilment rather than fulfilment through personal life such as home and leisure activities	22.1 (17)[c]	19.2 (10)[c]
b. Fulfilment through personal life such as home and leisure activities rather than through job	77.9 (60)	80.8 (42)

Notes: % (N) = percentage and number of respondents who chose a or b as their preferred response. A superscript letter beside the number of people indicates a significant difference between the proportion of women or men choosing a or b, as a result of chi-squared testing. c = $p < .001$, d = $p < .01$. Respondents: men and women in their mid-twenties.
Source: Compiled from Suzuki 2004, Table 2.1.

per cent of people, and males and females who agreed that 'women ought to take child-care leave and not quit their jobs even if they do give birth' topped fifty per cent (Asahi Shimbun 2004). There has been an increase in people who regard women's continuing in their jobs even during child-rearing, if they have the intention and will to work, as a regular path of career development.

In a survey relating to work and leisure time, 'work-oriented' responses have swiftly fallen since 1973, and, in 2003, the 'balance between work and leisure' response had significantly increased (see Table 1.4). This attitude change is especially pronounced among young women and men (aged sixteen to twenty-nine years). What is shown by this survey, as well as the trend towards emphasis on fulfilment in private life which I indicated in the previous section, is that while both men and women still value work for the sake of survival and self-realisation, they aspire to a life which is not work-centred, but which has a balance between employment and private life, including family and leisure: in short, a work/life balance.

The dual-income orientation of young people
If an economic recession causes instability in employment; an increase in male non-regular employees; a performance-based widening of the income disparity among men; the collapse of the lifetime employment system; and a deceleration of growth in husbands' pay, then the economic merits of wives staying at work inflate. In Japan, where a recession had endured since the 1990s until just recently (though there have been some signs of economic recovery since the beginning of 2006), eighty-three per cent of single women and men aged between twenty-five and thirty-five said that, if they were to marry: 'Given a choice, I would prefer us both to work,' while only seventeen per cent said: 'I would like only one of us to work'—showing an overwhelming preference for dual incomes (Nihon Keizai Shimbun 2004a).

Top place among reasons for supporting the idea of husband and wife both working was occupied by economic reasons such as a desire for a double income in anticipation of greater income stability, a wish to increase savings and have more leeway in life, and to maintain an affluent consumer lifestyle and higher-quality living standards. In fact, household income was twenty-five per cent greater in dual-income households than in those where only the husband worked (Nihon Keizai Shimbun 2004a). Moreover, if women in permanent jobs quit in mid-career for marriage or child-care, they not only carry the huge expense of raising children, but also forgo the pay they would later have received. Additional factors such as the rising divorce rate enhance the need for women's financial independence, and thus promote job-retention. A rise in women's individual economic status becomes a great driving force boosting awareness of gender equality (Yamaguchi 1999), and this, in turn, improves the Japanese social system and laws, becoming a momentum for the creation of an environment more conducive to work.

Elevation of young women's work motivation and job diversification
Among women in general, including those of middle-age and older, there has been a rise in the willingness to work and an extension in the years women continue working (see Table 1.2). Examination of the results of cohort analysis relating to women's actual and latent labour participation rates shows that the will to work intensifies in

inverse proportion to age. Conversely, in the case of men, both actual and latent participation rates have fallen in almost all age-groups, and the will to work is particularly low in young males aged between their late twenties and mid-thirties (Kōsei Rōdōshō Koyō Kintō/Jidō Katei-kyoku 2004).

In regard to the desire for advancement, the percentage of new female company recruits (aged between eighteen and twenty-two) aspiring to key positions (total of section chief, division chief, director and company president) showed an upward trend from 8.0 per cent in 1976 to 21.2 per cent in 2003 (Kōsei Rōdōshō Koyō Kintō/Jidō Katei-kyoku 2004). The proportion of males who desire advancement is about sixty per cent, much higher than that of females, but time-series analysis shows it to be somewhat on the downside.

Young working women with the desire for advancement have a higher egalitarian gender-role attitude than women wanting professional jobs or those without a wish for advancement (Suzuki 1991; Suzuki 1996). The psychological attributes of females in management positions are job-positivity, strength of intention to continue work, prioritisation of work over private life, and a high egalitarian gender-role attitude (Sano and Wakabayashi 1990). In the context of an advancing trend towards higher education for women and an increase in females with egalitarian gender-role attitude, the elevation in young women's willingness to work and desire for advancement suggests that there is a swelling reserve of women to take up managerial positions in future.

On the other hand, there has also been an increase in women taking up new types of work as entrepreneurs, free agents, or independent contractors, without belonging to any organisation (Suzuki 2006a). As their jobs principally are performed at satellite offices or at home, travelling time to their workplace is short, and they can manage their time themselves, making it easier for them to juggle job and home. This is a way of working in which they freely pursue their own success and self-realisation, without belonging to an organisation which has hierarchical relationships of bosses and subordinates. Then again, highly specialised knowledge, skills, ability and enthusiasm are necessary in order to carry on independently and self-responsibly in an unstable situation. Thanks to the progressive trend among females to gain higher education and the increase in those with specialised knowledge, growing numbers of women are expected to participate in the labour force under such new working arrangements from here on.

Changes in gender-role attitudes: heightened egalitarianism

In the past three to four decades, Japanese attitudes refuting the gendered division of labour have intensified, and egalitarian gender-role attitudes have risen (Suzuki 2006b) (see Table 1.9). Unlike in the case of attitudes towards career development, there is gender disparity in the level of gender-role egalitarianism, women's being the higher (Suzuki 1991) (see Table 1.10). Though formal equality in such areas as the legal system has gradually been put into shape, neither men nor women report a strong sense that substantive equality in society overall, or equality as a result of this action, has been achieved (see Table 1.11). There exists a contradiction, in that both the workplace and the home remain places of inequality, in spite of the value of gender equality having been taught continuously in Japan since the end of World War II (Yamaguchi 1999). Awareness of gender equality is weak in such public spheres as politics, conventional wisdom, customs, traditions, and in society as a whole (see Table 1.11).

According to an international comparative survey in 2002 on awareness of equality in the status of females and males (Naikakufu Danjo Kyōdō Sankaku-kyoku 2002) (see Table 1.11), women had a weaker awareness of equality in all fields, in all seven countries targeted except the Philippines. Generally speaking, there were also many countries in which awareness of equality was weak in the fields of politics and the workplace. A Japanese characteristic, similar to that of Korea, consisted of a weak awareness of equality in conventional wisdom, customs, traditions, and in society as a whole.

The low degree of attainment of equality in Japanese society overall is shown by its low GEM (Gender Empowerment Measure: an

Table 1.9: Youth attitudes towards gendered division of labour: 5-country comparison (%)

Country	Agree	Disagree	Don't know
Japan (1977)	50.4	31.7	17.8
Japan (2003)	16.1	68.5	15.4
Korea	14.1	79.0	6.9
United States	17.0	76.1	6.8
Sweden	3.7	92.6	3.7
Germany	22.7	72.0	5.2

Notes: Responses to: 'Men should be the breadwinner, and women should mind the home.' Respondents: men and women aged 18–24.
Source: Compiled from Naikakufu 2004, Figures 7.8 and 7.9.

Table 1.10: Gender comparison of egalitarian gender-role attitudes by SESRA-S

Item	Men (76)	Women (52)	t-value
1. Women should not take high level or high paying jobs because they interfere with marriage. #	4.14 (0.95)	4.53 (0.95)	2.25[a]
2. A husband should make the important decisions. #	4.12 (1.03)	4.55 (0.72)	2.78[b]
3. A working wife tends to neglect her husband, which increases the risk of divorce. #	4.05 (0.94)	4.60 (0.66)	3.84[c]
4. A woman's place is in the home; a man's place is in the office. #	4.30 (0.83)	4.63 (0.69)	2.46[a]
5. Working women put a strain on the family. #	4.08 (0.91)	4.38 (0.77)	1.99[a]
6. After getting married, a wife should not necessarily take her husband's name	3.38 (1.30)	3.94 (0.85)	2.94[b]
7. Domestic chores should be shared between husband and wife.	4.17 (0.93)	4.42 (0.72)	1.64
8. Bringing up children is the most important job for a woman. #	3.13 (0.91)	3.50 (0.85)	2.30[a]
9. It is extremely important to raise a boy to be masculine and a girl to be feminine. #	2.97 (1.19)	3.83 (0.94)	4.33[c]
10. Girls should be brought up to work in the home and boys outside the home. #	4.07 (1.04)	4.65 (0.62)	4.00[c]
11. Women should work part-time rather than full-time because they have to work in the home and bring up the children. #	3.92 (0.99)	4.19 (1.01)	1.51
12. For a woman, the roles of wife and mother are important, but working outside is equally important.	3.71 (0.99)	3.98 (0.94)	1.55
13. Women should continue working even after they have had children.	3.42 (0.77)	3.56 (0.83)	0.96
14. A woman should not work unless it is for economic reasons. #	3.34 (1.08)	3.77 (1.15)	2.14[a]
15. Women should not have jobs requiring major responsibilities or take highly competitive jobs because they have to work in the home and bring up children. #	3.70 (1.07)	4.06 (0.98)	1.94
Mean of total scores (SD)	56.51 (8.86)	62.69 (6.61)	4.28[c]
Mean of item scores (SD)	3.77 (0.59)	4.18 (0.44)	4.51[c]

Notes: 1. SESRA-S: Scale of Egalitarian Sex Role Attitudes–Short Form (Suzuki 1991). Likert-type 5-point scale. Possible scores ranged from fifteen to seventy-five in value. 2. Mean score (SD). 3. 'Marriage/married' includes de facto relationships. 4. Items followed by a # symbol are reverse-worded items. The means of reverse-worded items in the table show the results post-reversal, and therefore a higher score demonstrates a stronger degree of disagreement with the item content. 5. Respondents: men and women in their mid-twenties. 6. a = p <.05, b = p <.01, c = p <.001.

Source: Suzuki 2004, Table 3.4.

Table 1.11: *7-country comparison of awareness of gender equality by field: percentages regarding status of men and women as equal (%)*

	School education		Home life		Laws & systems		Workplace	
	M	W	M	W	M	W	M	W
Japan	70.3	65.5	48.2	34.0	45.9	27.2	31.7	21.1
Korea	62.8	57.2	37.4	26.4	26.2	8.5	25.4	16.4
Philippines	80.0	78.5	66.8	65.3	70.6	66.5	46.9	50.5
United States	59.4	55.9	46.1	39.1	43.6	35.6	34.3	23.0
Sweden	47.2	33.3	43.7	28.1	53.1	36.1	25.7	11.5
Germany	62.8	62.9	53.6	38.6	67.9	66.2	29.7	11.4
United Kingdom	61.2	64.3	52.0	42.3	50.1	48.3	35.5	26.8

	Politics		Conventional wisdom & customs		Society as a whole	
	M	W	M	W	M	W
Japan	21.4	11.4	19.7	14.3	23.3	12.1
Korea	5.5	3.5	7.7	3.2	12.0	5.0
Philippines	43.5	52.0	70.3	72.0	74.3	76.0
United States	16.6	9.4	39.0	26.5	33.2	23.3
Sweden	24.1	10.3	28.3	13.8	28.2	10.3
Germany	19.6	9.4	41.5	31.6	37.4	18.4
United Kingdom	24.4	14.0	49.6	45.4	44.2	39.3

Notes: M = men; W = women. Ratio of people who feel that genders are equal.
Respondents: men and women aged 20–59.
Source: Compiled from Naikakufu Danjo Kyōdō Sankaku-kyoku 2002, pp. 23–48.

index of female occupational and societal participation) (Japan ranking forty-third out of eighty countries) (Kokuren Kaihatsu Keikaku 2006). There are few organisations or firms with the willingness to accept women proactively and make full use of their abilities, and the proportion of female managers is also low. There is a particular shortage of fit receptacles for women with high educational qualifications (graduates of university or graduate school). In spite of there being large numbers of highly-educated women who wish to take advantage of their experience and ability by being re-hired as regular employees (Takeishi 2001), their latent needs are not being met because of the scarcity of firms that seek to hire them. By contrast with female university graduates in middle- to high age-groups, who tend strongly towards housewifisation, young university-educated women lean more towards career-orientation (Hara and Seiyama 2005, Suzuki 2004).

In Japanese society, where it is expected that declining fertility and the ageing of society will cause a shortage of labour in the near future, any failure to take full advantage of the labour power of women in general—not to mention that of young, highly-educated females with a powerful motivation to acquire specialist capabilities and to contribute to society—would represent an enormous cultural, social and economic loss.

Filling the gap between gender-role attitudes and the social system

During the past thirty to forty years, the attitude of Japanese women and men towards gender roles has certainly changed in the direction of independent orientation, equality-mindedness and diversity-mindedness, and gender norms have gained flexibility. In this period, the values of individualism have simultaneously permeated society, the object which people seek having changed from a way of life that emphasises conventional gender roles to one which places importance on personal choice as an individual. As we have seen in the previous section, the various tendencies towards change are pronounced among young people.

Nevertheless, as I have illustrated throughout this chapter, such change in people's attitudes has not yet obliterated the values of the gendered division of labour prominent in the systems and practices of Japanese culture, society, business and the family. Because improvements to systems and policies have not caught up with people's attitudinal changes and attitudinal diversification, individuals' margin for choice of ways of working and ways of life are narrow, and their degree of freedom is limited. Most women and men who aim for life career development are still in the position of having to choose only one out of two alternatives—work or home—and the pathway to a balance between the two is not yet in sight (Suzuki 2006a). No brake is yet to be applied to the widening of the gap due to the polarisation of workers into regular and non-regular employees. At last, in recent years, the treatment of non-regular employees has been improved, and a career-path leading to their hiring as regular employees has only just become visible.

The quest now is to create a society that will increase the degree of freedom in the workplace environment and acknowledge diverse ways of working, give fair treatment and appraisal, and achieve a work/life balance. This does not mean that women would adopt without modification the current working style and lifestyle of men in permanent jobs. In order for any worker to build an autonomous life career—whether they be male or female, married or single, regular or non-regular employees, Japanese or non-Japanese—it is vital that they be able to work under fair conditions of systems of social security, taxation, employment and wages (Suzuki 2006a). A favourable outcome can also be anticipated for enterprises, as improvement in employees' quality of life and greater life satisfaction will mean lowered stress and heightened productivity. One might add that in these times of a progressively-declining birth-rate, it is essential for firms fully to implement measures to assist employees in juggling child-rearing and work. It is even more important, however, for companies to bring to fruition policies which would achieve a broad-ranging balance between private life and work; and to secure a variety of capable personnel who are eager to work, by establishing a fair personnel-evaluation system.

2 Work, Child-rearing and Gender: Psychological Distress in Women with Pre-schooler Children in Japan

Akihide Inaba

Introduction

It is widely known that Japan is a country characterised by a strongly gendered division of labour. In the public sphere, the presence of the gendered division of labour has been indicated by women's low participation rate in the labour market, wage inequity and so on, and by husbands' low participation in household work or child-rearing, in the private sphere. There is no doubt that Japanese society has had both constraints in behaviour choices and many inequalities associated with gender, and such gendered division has undoubtedly constituted an important element that characterises Japanese society at large. An appreciation of any changes in the gendered division of labour is thus imperative for understanding social change in Japan, and has very important meaning.

Now, it has been reported that the female participation rate in the labour market is increasing, while wage inequalities between men and women are gradually decreasing (Kōsei Rōdōshō Koyō Kintō/Jidō Katei-kyoku 2004). On that point, it may be argued that the gender-inequality structure in the public sphere has been changing in the direction of equality. On the other hand, however, the rate of employed women's retirement due to childbirth has remained high. For example, only thirty per cent of full-time, regularly-employed women continue to work after childbirth (Iwasawa 2003), and these figures have not changed in recent years (Tanaka 1996). Thus, we can say that either the gendered division of labour in Japan has changed, or not, as the case may be, depending on what we see as an essential condition for such a division, but at least we *can* state that there have been difficult conditions for women continuing to work for the duration of their child-rearing stage.

In such conditions, what is the actual state of regularly-employed women's well-being? Sociologically, we can evoke two images for them:

one is the image that they are exhausted by role-overload from their dual role of work and care for their family, and that they are experiencing low well-being. This is a figure which Arlie Hochschild has termed 'stalled revolution' (Hochschild 1989), in that role-overload has emerged for employed women because only the gendered division in the public sphere becomes equal, contrary to that of the private sphere, where it does not become equal. If this be true, then these working women with children may be supposed to experience a worse psychological state than homemaker wives.

The contrasting image is that employed women are experiencing a better psychological state than their stay-at-home counterparts. Provided that conditions made women's employment compatible with child-rearing, it would be difficult to predict role-overload for them, and they would be able to obtain various benefits from employment. This position is based on the role-expansion theory (Thoits 1983) which insists that having roles brings one a sense of social identity, or other gratification.

Our study examines both of the above-mentioned patterns and changes in the well-being of married women with pre-school children, by using two, large, repeated cross-sectional datasets from surveys conducted in 1999 and 2004 (NFRJ98, NFRJ03) in Japan. Our analyses will show the present state of regularly-employed women who have pre-school children (including babies or infants) in Japan, and will also show the direction of change. We next examine the factors which regulate these women's well-being and changes in these factors. These analyses will promote an understanding of the necessary conditions for gender-equalisation in present-day Japan.

Well-being of working mothers with pre-schoolers

Patterns of well-being

Previous studies regarding this theme in the United States basically tended to stress the psychological advantage to women of employment. In fact, many empirical studies have reported better well-being among employed women and poorer well-being among female homemakers (Ross, Mirowsky and Huber 1983; Mirowsky and Ross 1989; Umberson and Williams 1999; Lennon 1999; Simon 2002). This is thought to be the result of homemaker women overly committing to child-rearing, and being obliged to experience social isolation (Umberson and Williams 1999).

By contrast, studies of married women with children have shown that employed women's well-being becomes worse if they do not have sufficient arrangements for child-care, or if their husband's participation in household work or child-rearing is low (Mirowsky and Ross 1989). In a review of studies in the 1980's, McLanahan and Adams (1987) pointed out that women's employment had a great psychological advantage for women, but that gender inequality at home made it difficult for women to receive such an advantage. Generally, it seems possible to surmise that employment initially has a psychological advantage for women, but once they experience role-overload, such an advantage will disappear.

In Japan, Inaba (1999a) examined patterns of family role strain (i.e. a sense of role-overload, sense of role-captivity, and so on) among married women who lived in a metropolitan area and had pre-school children, but neither regularly-employed women nor homemakers showed high role-strain. Nishimura (2004 2005) also analysed the sense of role-overload among married women by using large representative data from Japan (NFRJ98), finding that a sense of role-overload tended to be high among women whose youngest child was aged seven to nineteen, rather than women with a pre-schooler. Nishimura assumed the operation of this mechanism because women who had retired by childbirth began to resume work at this stage and had experienced a sense of role-overload (Nishimura 2005). These studies suggest that the mental health of regularly-employed women with pre-school children is not particularly bad. If we synthesise these findings with our initial discussion, we can assume the presence of social-selection effects, in that only in a fulfilled condition do women choose regular employment in this stage. What, then, constitutes a 'good condition'?

Enabling compatibility of child-rearing with regular employment

In the United States, a primary factor taken by sociologists as enabling women with children to work is their husbands' participation in household work and child-rearing. In fact, Mirowsky and Ross (1989) showed that the well-being of regularly-employed women with children improved greatly when their husbands shared child-care.

In Japan, however, men's participation in household work and child-rearing is generally low, and although the husbands of regularly-employed wives participate in household work more than the husbands of homemakers, men's entire level of participation is still extremely low (Nagai 1992; Matsuda 2004; Matsuda 2006). How, then, do we reconcile this contradiction—husbands' low participation in household work, yet the 'not-so-bad' mental health of employed wives?

Inaba (1999b) examined this problem, but husbands' participation in household work and child-rearing did not show any ameliorating effects on family role-strain among regularly-employed women. The factor which did ameliorate role-strain was the existence of wives' extended family with which the wives could leave their children in an emergency. Most of the regularly-employed women with pre-school children had such relatives, and wives who did not have such relatives experienced high strain.

In other words, as household work or child-rearing were shared within a loose network constituted by wives, day-care centres (*hoikujo*) and relatives, husbands' small commitment to household work and child-rearing *per se* did not therefore directly cause wives' role-strain. What is directly related to women's sense of role-strain seems to be whether they have someone with whom they can leave their children when those children are sick. As most of the children's day-care centres in Japan do not accept a child if he or she is unwell, if the child's parents do not have such relatives available, then either the husband or wife has to be absent from work.

If unable to obtain any cooperation from their husbands, wives seem to feel severe role-strain. This scenario is not peculiar to Japan, however, as Belsky and Kelly (1994) have pointed out almost the same story in the case of American couples. In both Japan and the United States, though the most difficult situation for balancing child-rearing and work commonly seems to be the time when children are sick, the function of the kin network seems more important in Japan both at usual and unusual times.

Theoretically, if the functions of the kin network are great, husbands' low participation in household work or child-rearing will not cause particularly much conflict to wives. Notably, the better the kin network functions, the higher will be the possibility that the traditional gendered division of labour will be maintained. Conversely, if parents do not depend on a kin network (or do not have an available network), or if a couple is isolated from its kin network, then husbands' participation in household work or child-rearing, or husbands' ability to substitute for their wives, must have critical meaning.

Contrary to our prediction, we seldom see studies in Japan which report a significant effect upon a wife's well-being of her husband's participation in household work and child-rearing. Neither the research of Yamato (2006) nor Inaba (2005), who used data from a representative large sample, showed any significant effect upon a wife's marital satisfaction or psychological distress due to a husband's participation in household work.

We can thus assume the availability of a kin network to be an element constituting a 'fulfilled condition.'[1] As a result of gender-equalisation in the public realm, however, we can suppose that there will be an increase in women who wish to continue to work even if they do not have such a kin network. Such a change will mean an increase in women who ask their husbands to participate in household work or child-rearing, or to substitute for them when their children are sick (to take special nursing leave, for example, or have a day off work). Considering the above, we can predict that husbands' participation in household work and child-rearing, or their substitution for their wives when their children are ill, will gradually have an effect upon the wives.

This does not mean, though, that the effect of a husband upon his wife is limited only to his participation (or lack thereof) in household work or child-rearing. Previous studies show that expressive support from husband to wife has a large effect upon the wife's marital satisfaction or psychological distress (Inaba 2005; Yamato 2006). Generally, it is said that spousal support is the most crucial among all of the various kinds of social support (Thoits 1995), and it has also already been reported in Japan that social support such as a husband's positive evaluation of his wife's ability or a husband's lending an ear to his wife's worries is related to lower psychological distress (Inaba 2005). Inaba (2005) examined psychological distress among regularly-employed women with pre-school children by using NFRJ98 data, and concluded that a husband's caring for his wife who did the household work and child-rearing (that is, caring for her career) had more of an effect upon both the wife's psychological distress and family role-strain than his sharing household work and child-rearing.

A popular statement says: 'If a woman wants to continue working during her child-rearing stage, it is imperative for her to have an especially sympathetic husband.' If this be true, we can also predict that regularly-employed wives will have more expressive support than other wives. Let us therefore examine the possibility of expressive support from a husband constituting a 'fulfilled condition.'

Effects of social policy

If we study the changes in the gendered division of labour in Japan, it is necessary simultaneously to consider the effects of recent social policy. As the Basic Law for a Gender-Equal Society (*Danjo kyōdō sankaku shakai kihon hō*) was enforced in 1999, it resulted in policies for gender equalisation in various realms being facilitated by the Japanese government. Concretely, local government became able actively to administer policies toward gender equalisation, such as raising the proportion of female representatives in local government, setting up shelters for victims of domestic violence, holding various lectures to enlighten the public about a gender-equal society, subsidising social research for verifying gender equalisation, and so on.

On the other hand, below-replacement fertility (*shōshika*) came to be realised as a critical political issue after the late 1990s in Japan. Policies for countering below-replacement fertility are literally equal to policies for raising fertility, so logically these do not accord with policies for gender-equalisation, but it has been stressed that gender-equalisation is necessary as one of the policies for responding to below-replacement fertility. In the midst of such trends, the Japanese government has been adopting policies for men to facilitate their participation in child-rearing or the taking of parental leave, and has been honouring 'family-friendly' companies.

Thus, after 2000 in Japan, policies for gender-equalisation seem to have been synchronised with policies for addressing below-replacement fertility, and we cannot dismiss as insignificant these policy-effects upon the gendered division of labour. Theoretically, it is natural to assume that married women tend to request their husband's participation in household work and child-rearing, and also that there seems to be an increase in women who hope to work during their child-rearing stage, irrespective of having an available kin network.

Research questions and hypotheses

Let us specify the research questions and the hypotheses used in this study. First, this study examines the patterns of married women's well-being by using two repeated cross-sectional data-sets. The main object of the study is the well-being of regularly-employed married women with pre-school children, but, in order to clarify these women's psychological state, we try to compare them with women of a different employment status and life-stage. We could propose two opposite hypotheses for regularly-employed women with pre-schoolers. If we follow the role-overload hypothesis which assumes that the regular employment of women brings them role-overload, then the well-being of regularly-employed women will turn out to be worse than that of other women. Contrary to this, if we follow the role-expansion hypothesis which assumes that the regular employment of women brings them various advantages, then the well-being of regularly-employed women will turn out to be better than that of other women.

Logically, however, this role-expansion hypothesis is possible only if there are conditions which prevent role-overload. For a woman who is in a condition of experiencing role-overload, it is difficult to approve of the role-expansion hypothesis unless the woman concerned gains new conditions or otherwise gives up working. In the opposite case, if women's wish to continue working becomes stronger, and if they choose to continue working, regardless of the availability of support, we can predict the occurrence of role-overload and an increase in women who experience lower well-being.

Considering as such, we can posit the following general hypothesis and some specific hypotheses in a concrete context:

Hypothesis 1: Regular employment enhances the well-being of a married woman only if she has the conditions to prevent role-overload.

According to this hypothesis, the critical factors are 'factors that prevent role-overload.' Regarding such factors, we can posit the following specific hypotheses:

Hypothesis 2: Kin support for household work or child-rearing enhances the well-being of regularly-employed women.

Hypothesis 3: Husbands' participation in household work or child-rearing enhances the well-being of regularly-employed women.

Both of these hypotheses assume that sharing daily work (household work or child-rearing) prevents the occurrence of role-overload. It is also possible to posit further hypotheses in non-daily situations, as below:

Hypothesis 4: Availability of kin to whom they can leave children in emergencies enhances the well-being of regularly-employed women.

Hypothesis 5: A husband's substitutability in looking after children in an emergency enhances the well-being of regularly-employed women.

As previously mentioned, in a society where kin have large functions, we predict that both Hypothesis 2 and Hypothesis 4 will be supported, but both Hypothesis 3 and Hypothesis 5 will not necessarily be supported. If a couple is highly independent of kin, and if the wife's orientation for gender-equalisation is high, both Hypothesis 3 and 5 are predicted to be supported. Therefore, after 2000, when the achievement of a 'gender-equal society' was facilitated as a Japanese governmental policy, we can predict that the effects of both Hypothesis 3 and 5 will have been increasing.

Additionally, it is well-known that not only instrumental support such as sharing household participation or child-rearing, but expressive support, also, has a great impact on married women's well-being. In this regard, we can only use spousal support in our data-sets, so we posit the following hypothesis:

Hypothesis 6: Expressive support from a husband enhances the well-being of a regularly-employed wife.

Method

Data

We use two representative public data-sets in Japan: NFRJ98 (National Family Research of Japan 1998) and NFRJ03 (National Family Research of Japan 2003). Both of these are repeated cross-sectional data consisting of a self-administered questionnaire, conducted by the Japan Society of Family Sociology (Nihon Kazoku Shakai Gakkai).[2]

The NFRJ98 data were collected in 1999. This data-set consists of 6,985 respondents out of 10,500 persons (women and men, aged twenty-eight to seventy-seven, born between 1921 and 1970), sampled by a stratified random sampling of Japanese (Watanabe, Inaba and Shimazaki 2004). The NFRJ03 data, on the other hand, were collected in 2004. This data-set consists of 6,308 respondents out of 10,000 persons (men and women, aged twenty-eight to seventy-seven, born between 1926 and 1975), sampled by a stratified random sampling of Japanese (Nihon Kazoku Shakaigakkai Zenkoku Kazoku Chōsa Iinkai 2005).

Though these two data-sets are cross-sectional, both of them are examples of the few representative data-sets in Japan with a large sample size and many variables relevant for family research. As both data-sets had a small sample size for both husbands temporarily-employed and husbands having no job when the couple had children, we excluded these respondents (this means that the husband's employment status in our sample was either 'regularly-employed' or 'self-employed').

In analyses of descriptive patterns of distress, we set as our respondents only married women. Women with children were divided into four groups by age of youngest child: aged zero to six (pre-school), aged seven to twelve (elementary school), aged thirteen to eighteen (junior- and senior high school), and aged nineteen to twenty-four. This means that we limited our respondents to those with children aged zero to twenty-four years. For the sake of comparison with women without children, we established childless married women who had been married for ten years or less as the 'childless' group. We compared the mean score differences in distress among these five children's age-groups by the wife's employment status. Hypothesis testing was done through analysis of regularly-employed women with children aged zero to six years. In our analysis, we set up homemaker women with children aged zero to six years as a comparison group.

Measures

Dependent Variable

One measure of well-being is the Center for Epidemiological Studies Depression Scale (CES–D), which is a well-known scale for measuring people's psychological distress (depression) (Simon 2002). Because CES–D items in NFRJ98 and NFRJ03 are a little different from each other, we used eleven items common to each data set.

These items were:

> We would like to ask you about your physical or mental state <u>during the past week</u>. How often did you experience each of the following feelings or matters? Circle your answer to each item:
> • I was bothered by things which usually don't bother me;

- I felt that I could not shake off the blues, even if my family or friends cheered me up;
- I felt depressed;
- I had trouble keeping my mind on what I was doing;
- My appetite decreased;
- I felt that everything I did was an effort;
- I felt fearful;
- I had trouble sleeping;
- I talked less than usual;
- I felt lonely without company;
- I felt sad.

Possible responses were 1 = not at all, 2 = one or two days a week, 3 = three or four days a week, and 4 = almost every day. Possible scores ranged from eleven to forty-four in value. We excluded 'Yes tendency' samples by ruling out respondents who scored all items (not shown here) the same—because one reverse item was included, we could judge a 'Yes tendency' when all of the items were equal. The internal consistency of the scale was .88 for NFRJ98, and .87 for NFRJ03 (Cronbach's alpha).

Independent Variables
We set up the six variables below as independent variables corresponding to our hypotheses.

Husbands' participation in household work
We used three items to assess the frequency of a husband's household work per week, namely: 'preparing meals,' 'washing clothes,' and 'cleaning the bathroom' for NFRJ98, and 'preparing meals,' 'washing clothes,' and 'cleaning the house' for NFRJ03. The response categories were: 'almost never; once a week; twice or three times a week; four or five times a week; almost every day' for NFRJ98, and 'almost never; one day a week; two or three days a week; four or five days a week; six or seven days a week' for NFRJ03.

Husbands' participation was so scant, however, that the distributions of each item were highly skewed. To deal with this problem, we recoded each response as 1 if the husband participated to any extent (i.e. greater than or equal to one day a week), and 0 if the husband did not participate at all. We then added these three items to produce an indicator.

Participation in child-rearing

We measured the participation in child-rearing by using a single item: 'taking care of children or grandchildren' in NFRJ98, and also 'looking after children' in NFRJ03. Both of these items were assessed by the same five-point scale. Unlike household work, however, men's participation in child-rearing was rather high, so we converted each response into the number of days per week (i.e. 0, 1, 2.5, 4.5, 6.5) as a score.

Availability of parental support

In NFRJ98, the place of residence of both the wife's and husband's parents (father and mother) was assessed by six categories: 'co-residence; next-door or in a house within the same site; within walking distance; less than one hour's journey away; less than three hours' journey away; and, greater than or equal to three hours' journey away.' In NFRJ03, 'next-door or in a house within the same site' was divided into 'another house within the same site' and 'the house next door,' so that seven categories were used. For both data sets, we assigned 1 if the respondent had at least one parent within walking distance; otherwise, we assigned 0 as a dummy variable.

Availability of a husband's emergency assistance

Under the question: 'When you need help or person to talk to in the following situations, who, or which agency, do you depend upon? Please circle the applicable responses. (You may circle as many as necessary.),' we set up an item: 'When you need emergency assistance for sickness or accident,' for NFRJ98; and 'When you need emergency assistance because you or a family member become ill or have an accident,' for NFRJ03.

For each item, eleven relationship categories were listed, and respondents were asked to answer regarding every relationship as to whether they could count on that person's help. Responses were coded 1 if the respondent could count on that person and 0 if they could not. If the spouse (husband) was selected, then the emergency assistance of the husband was coded 1; otherwise, 0 as a dummy variable.

Emergency assistance of parents

With the same items as emergency assistance of the husband, we coded 1 if a category 'parents or a sibling' was selected in NFRJ98, and also coded 1 if at least either the respondent's 'own parent' or 'spouse's parent' was selected in NFRJ03. Otherwise, we coded 0 for both as dummy variables. In NFRJ98, 'parents' share a response category with 'siblings,' so we made up a category consisting of the respondent's or spouse's parents, her own siblings, and her spouse's siblings, though the results of analysis did not show any substantial difference.

Husband's expressive support
The items for this variable were identical both in NFRJ98 and NFRJ03: 'my spouse listens to my anxieties and worries; my spouse evaluates my ability and effort highly; and, my spouse gives me suggestions and advice.' For each item, the response was assessed by a four-point scale: 'applicable' (= 4); 'rather applicable' (= 3); 'rather not applicable' (= 2); and 'not applicable' (= 1). We then summed up these three items as an indicator. The internal consistency of the scale was .84 for NFRJ98, and .87 for NFRJ03 (Cronbach's alpha).

Control variables
As our sample sizes of regularly-employed women with children aged six or under were not very large, it was necessary to limit the number of control variables to a minimum. We thus chose the wife's age, wife's years of education, her having two or more children (a dummy variable, as the reference category was having only one child), and the wife being regularly-employed (a dummy variable, the reference category being a homemaker). Ideally, the household income of the past year also should have been used as a control variable, but as this variable was missing in many cases, and strongly correlated with the wife's years of education, we did not use this variable.

Strategies for the analyses

In the analyses regarding descriptive patterns of well-being, we would compare mean scores of distress among groups defined by the combination of the life-stage variable (age of youngest child) and women's employment status.

With regard to the hypotheses, as Hypothesis 1 appears as the result of Hypotheses 2 to 6, it turns out that this study directly examines Hypotheses 2 to 6. These hypotheses relate to women with children, so we limited our sample only to women with children aged six or under (pre-schoolers). As mentioned above, we limited our sample to women either regularly-employed or who were homemakers. The reasons were: 1) both the temporarily-employed and self-employed were few in number; 2) comparison of regularly-employed women with homemakers would make clear the meaning of the interaction effect; and 3) in so far as the homemaker is the mode category of women with pre-school children, and regularly-employed women are predicted to increase in future, comparison between them would have much theoretical significance.

If Hypothesis 2 to Hypothesis 6 are supported both for the regularly-employed and homemakers, independent variables in the hypotheses must show a significant main effect. If the effect is unique to the regularly-employed, we can expect a significant interaction effect of an independent variable with regular employment. In cases where the significant main effect was shown, it turned out that the 'fulfilled condition' of regularly-employed women could be explained only if the distribution of that independent variable was significantly high (or low) for them. If a significant difference in the independent variable is not shown, the significant main effect does not explain the fulfilled condition of regularly-employed women.

In an examination of the hypotheses, we set psychological distress as a dependent variable and applied the basic model (OLS regression) consisting of control variables and the wife's regular employment (a dummy variable) as independent variables, at first. Next, we examined the interaction effect added to the basic model. The interaction effect was not examined by entering all interaction terms together, but by entering them one by one. However, if the interaction effect was not significant, we show only the results of the main effect model.

Well-being of married women with pre-school children

Patterns of well-being

Let us look at the descriptive pattern of well-being of married women with pre-school children. We show the mean scores of distress by age of youngest child and the wife's employment status, as Figure 2.1 for 1999, and as Figure 2.2 for 2004.

In Figure 2.1, it is very distinctive that the psychological distress of regularly-employed women with pre-schoolers is extremely low. Even though the distress of women with pre-schoolers is generally low, the distress of regularly-employed women is significantly the lowest among them. Distress is rather high among women with children aged seven to twelve, or thirteen to eighteen, and in these stages, regularly-

Figure 2.1: Mean scores of psychological distress by youngest child's age and women's employment status (NFRJ98)

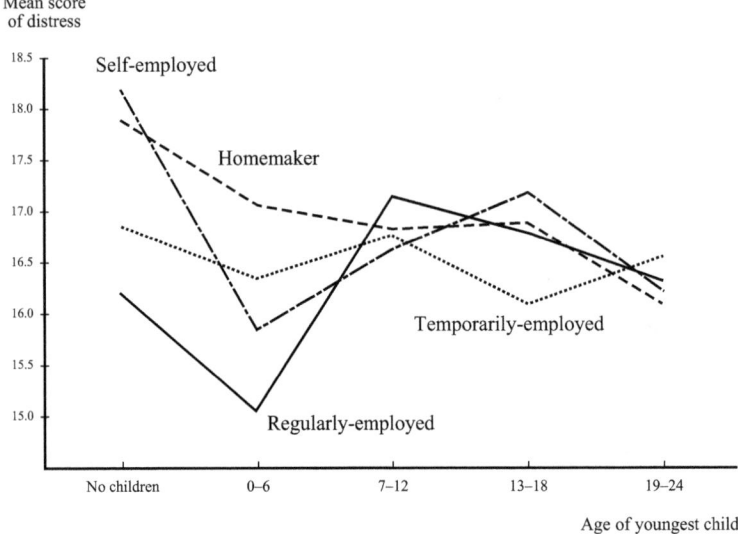

Figure 2.2: Mean scores of psychological distress by youngest child's age and women's employment status (NFRJ03)

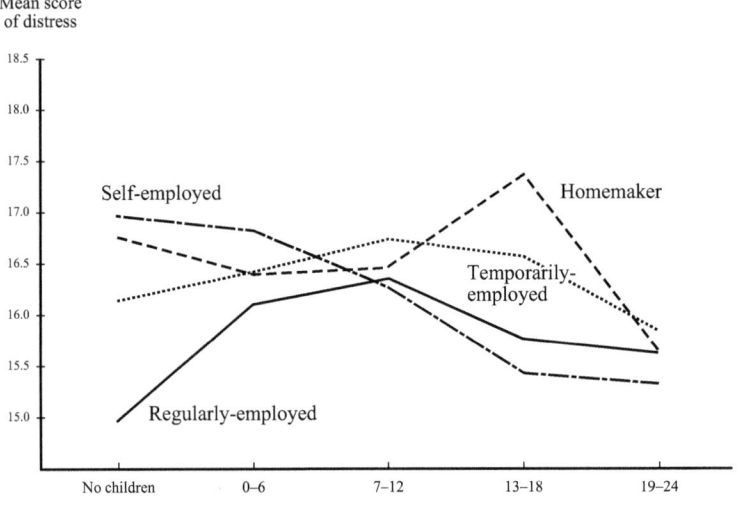

employed women also show a high distress score. From these results, at least it is difficult to retain images of regularly-employed wives as being exhausted by a double burden of child-rearing and work, or images of homemaker wives as experiencing lonely, stressful child-rearing.

In 2004, however, these tendencies become a little different. In that year, though married women's distress during the period in which their youngest child was aged six or under showed a similar general tendency to be low and distress during youngest child aged seven to twelve to be high, the low mean score of distress among regularly-employed women with pre-school children disappeared and the difference among women of various employment status had shrunk. For regularly-employed women, well-being was better in 1999 and rather worse in 2004. We can thus conclude as follows:

1. The well-being of married women with pre-school children is not far worse than in other stages.
2. The hypothesis that the well-being of regularly-employed women with pre-school children is worse cannot be supported.
3. The role-expansion hypothesis of employment held true in 1999, but neither the role-overload hypothesis nor the role-expansion hypothesis was supported in 2004.

Factors affecting well-being

Let us examine Hypotheses 2 to 6. Descriptive statistics of the variables are shown in Table 2.1. For comparison, we show figures for the regularly-employed and homemakers separately, both for 1999 and 2004.

Though participation in household work by the husbands of regularly-employed women is significantly higher than that of homemaker women for both time-points, their participation *per se* is not so high, as long as we see the mean scores.

'Participation in household work' means the number of household work items. Figures were at an extremely low level in 1999, however, and even husbands of the regularly-employed showed only 0.3 work items. In 2004, both the husbands of regularly-employed women and those of homemakers showed significantly higher participation in household work than in 1999. Husbands' participation in household work seems to be increasing gradually, in general.

Contrary to this, participation in child-rearing in 2004 was rather low. Because one item in 1999 was vaguely worded as 'taking care

Table 2.1: Descriptive statistics of regularly-employed wives and homemaker wives

	NFRJ98(1999)				NFRJ03(2004)			
	Regularly-employed (n = 42)		Homemaker (n = 184)		Regularly-employed (n = 51)		Homemaker (n = 282)	
	Mean	SD	Mean	SD	Mean	SD	Mean	SD
Age of youngest child	3.00	1.55	2.99	1.68	3.20c	1.83	2.37	1.91
Wife's years of education	13.33	1.68	13.10	1.44	13.45	1.65	13.15	1.54
Having more than two children (1)	0.57	0.50	0.71	0.46	0.69	0.47	0.67	0.47
Husband's participation in household work	0.33d	0.30	0.17	0.24	1.25d	1.09	0.60	0.81
Husband's participation in child-rearing	4.26d	2.69	2.47	2.25	3.36c	2.34	2.38	2.31
Proximity of wife's parents' home (1)	0.33d	0.48	0.17	0.38	0.20	0.40	0.16	0.36
Proximity of husband's parents' home (1)	0.33	0.48	0.34	0.48	0.37a	0.49	0.29	0.45
Proximity of parents' home (1)	0.64d	0.48	0.49	0.50	0.53a	0.50	0.43	0.50
Husband's emergency assistance (1)	0.71	0.46	0.73	0.45	0.67	0.48	0.59	0.49
Parent's emergency assistance (1)	0.83	0.38	0.88	0.33	0.84	0.37	0.84	0.36
Husband's emotional support	9.10	2.70	8.81	2.27	8.53	2.67	9.23	2.17
Distress	15.24b	3.81	17.29	5.07	15.76	4.60	16.52	4.74

Note: Significant tests are T tests of mean score differences between the employed wives and homemaker wives.
a = p < .10 b = p < .05 c = p < .01 d = p < .001

of children or grandchildren,' while its counterpart in 2004 was expressed as 'looking after children,' the difference may have been caused by the different wording of items. From this point, drawing inferences about the changes in participation in child-rearing activities seems problematic. Meanwhile, the husbands of regularly-employed women participate in child-rearing significantly more than do husbands of homemakers at both points.

With regard to the husband's emergency assistance, data in 1999 showed seventy-one per cent for the regularly-employed and seventy-four per cent for homemaker women, but in 2004, sixty-seven per cent and fifty-nine per cent, respectively. The figure showed a decreasing trend.

As for the matter of the availability of kin, the percentage of women who had kin within walking distance was sixty-four per cent for the regularly-employed and forty-nine per cent for homemakers in 1999. The possession rate of available kin was significantly higher for regularly-employed women. Moreover, when we classified parents as either the husband's or the wife's, the result showed that the possession rate of the husband's parents did not give rise to any significant difference between the two groups, but the possession rate of the wife's parents was thirty-three per cent for the regularly-employed and seventeen per cent for homemakers; regularly-employed women appeared to live near their parents. In 2004, however, these figures declined. Possession rates of kin within walking distance were fifty-three per cent for the regularly-employed and forty-three per cent for homemakers. We can assume an increase in regularly-employed women without kin living in close proximity.

Availability of kin in times of emergency was eighty-three per cent for the regularly-employed and eighty-eight per cent for homemakers in 1999, and eighty-four per cent for both the regularly-employed and homemakers in 2004. These figures equate to stating that more than eighty per cent of both the regularly-employed and homemakers can count on kin support in an emergency, and there is almost no difference between the regularly-employed and homemakers. Although the tendency to have kin within walking distance is higher for the regularly-employed than for homemakers, the function of kin is universally strong, irrespective of the wife's employment status. Previous studies have pointed out that many wives with pre-school children count on kin support (Inaba 1999b), and this corresponds with our findings.

Next, we did OLS regression analyses by setting variables supposed in the hypotheses as independent variables, and the wife's psychological distress as the dependent variable for both of the two time-points. We show these results as Table 2.2 for 1999 and as Table 2.3 for 2004.

In Table 2.2, we cannot find any substantially meaningful effects for independent variables. Though only a husband's expressive support has a significant main effect, expressive support itself was not significantly high for regularly-employed women. A significant main effect of regular employment was maintained after controlling expressive support. The distress of regularly-employed women in 1999 was extremely low, but our analyses could not find the factor causing such low distress. The higher the husband's expressive support, the lower was the wife's distress, and these patterns were observed both for the regularly-employed and homemakers.

In Table 2.3, availability of a husband's emergency assistance had a significant interaction effect with employment status (regularly-employed=1, homemaker=0). A parameter estimate of these variables was as follows:

2.28 Regularly-employed + 0.08 Husband's emergency assistance
− 4.82 Regularly-employed × Husband's emergency assistance
= (2.28 - 4.82 Husband's emergency assistance) × Regularly-employed + 0.08 Husband's emergency assistance

If the husband was counted, the expected value of regularly-employed women's distress (conditioned mean) was −2.54 lower than that of homemakers. If not counted, it was 2.28 higher than that of homemakers.

To sum up: if a wife could count on her husband's assistance in an emergency, her regular employment was associated with lower distress for her, but, if not, her regular employment tended to be associated with high distress. This is a result corresponding with Hypothesis 5. Additionally, albeit at a ten-per-cent significance level, a husband's participation in child-rearing corresponded to Hypothesis 3, and this showed a significant interaction effect with regular employment.

The direction of this effect was identical to the effect of a husband's emergency support. If her husband participates in child-rearing, a regularly-employed woman shows the same level of distress as a homemaker. If her husband does not participate, the distress of a regularly-employed woman is significantly higher than that of a homemaker. A husband's participation in child-rearing was related to distress only for a regularly-employed wife.

Table 2.2: OLS regression on wife's psychological distress (NFRJ98)

Independent variables	Unstandardised coefficient (β)								
	Model 1	Model 2	Model 3	Model 6	Model 7	M Model 8	Model 9
Step 1									
Intercept	13.61	13.36	14.16	13.48	14.35	13.47	18.27
Age of youngest child	0.06	0.07	0.03	0.07	0.05	0.06	-0.05
Wife's years of education	0.28	0.27	0.26	0.28	0.29	0.27	0.32
Having more than two children (1)	-0.29	-0.26	-0.34	-0.29	-0.33	-0.29	-0.29
Regularly-employed (1)	-2.04[b]	-2.22[b]	-1.56[a]	-2.08[b]	-2.07[b]	-2.02[b]	-1.70[b]
Step 2									
Husband's participation in household work		1.33					
Husband's participation in child-rearing			-0.06				
Proximity of parents' home (1)				0.27			
Husband's emergency assistance (1)					-1.14		
Parent's emergency assistance (1)						0.25	
Husband's emotional support							-0.55[d]
Step 3									
Regularly-employed × step 2		(2.00)	(0.23)	(-2.73)	(2.20)	(1.26)	(-0.15)
R^2	.031	.036	.024	.032	.042	.031	.09

Note: If step 3 is not significant, the coefficient of step 1 and step 2 shows the results of the main effect model.

a = < .10 b = < .05 c = p < .01 d = p < .01 n = 226

Table 2.3: OLS regression on wife's psychological distress (NFRJ03)

Independent variables	Unstandardised coefficient (β)								
	Model 1	Model 2	Model 3	Model 4	Model 5	Model 6	Model 7	Model 8	Model 9
Step 1									
Intercept	16.13	15.94	15.54	15.7	16.48	16.18	20.90
Age of youngest child	0.23	0.22	0.23	0.23	0.22	0.23	0.16
Wife's years of education	−0.01	0.02	0.02	0.01	−0.04	−0.01	0.08
Having more than two children (1)	0.01	0.02	0.04	−0.01	−0.09	0.01	−0.47
Regularly-employed (1)	−0.94	−0.67	0.99	−0.98	2.28[a]	−0.94	−1.32[a]
Step 2									
Husband's participation in household work		−0.42							
Husband's participation in child-rearing			0.07						
Proximity of parents' home (1)				0.34					
Husband's emergency assistance (1)					0.08				
Parent's emergency assistance (1)						−0.13			
Husband's emotional support									−.60[d]
Step 3									
Regularly-employed × step 2		(0.40)	−0.60[a]	(−0.49)	−4.82[c]	(−0.18)	(0.01)
R^2	.011	.017	.023	.013	.046	.012	0.091

Note: If step 3 is not significant, the coefficient of step 1 and step 2 shows the results of the main effect model.
a = < .10 b = < .05 c = p < .01 d = p < .01 n = 333

Contrary to our prediction, neither Hypothesis 2 nor Hypothesis 4 was upheld. Both the presence of kin within walking distance and the availability of kin support in an emergency had no significant effect on distress for both the main effect and interaction effect. A husband's expressive support, corresponding to Hypothesis 6, had only a significant main effect on distress, and had no significant interaction effect with regular employment as well, according to the results from the 1999 data.

Finally, after controlling for the husband's expressive support, we examined the interaction effects of regular employment both with a husband's emergency assistance and with his child-rearing, in terms of distress. Both significant interaction effects were maintained. We can observe that a husband's emergency assistance and a husband's participation in child-rearing had a larger effect in 2004. These factors affected only regularly-employed women, not homemakers. At both time-points, a husband's expressive support had a strong effect on distress for both the regularly-employed and the homemaker. We could reconfirm the important function of a husband's expressive support for women with pre-school children.

Discussion

The role of a husband's participation in housework and child-rearing

At both time-points, we could not observe any significant interaction effect of a husband's participation in household work with a wife's regular employment. As it appears on descriptive statistics, a husband's participation in daily household work is generally low, even if his wife is employed. We can consider these results as follows: (1) because the degree of participation in household work itself is generally low, the levels of participation do not have much meaning (even 'high' participation virtually means a 'low' level); (2) as household work is shared by kin or others, a husband's participation in household work itself is not so imperative. Though it is not possible to conclude which is true, a husband's low participation in household work itself does not seem to be a serious stressor for a wife even if she is regularly-employed.

Contrary to this, a husband's participation in child-rearing showed a weak interaction effect with a wife's regular employment in 2004. As regularly-employed wives came to expect their husband to participate in child-rearing, a husband's participation might have influence only for regularly-employed wives. Anyway, it is notable that the more recent the example, the ever greater effect husbands' participation in child-rearing had on their wives.

Husband's substitutability in emergencies

A husband's emergency assistance did not show any remarkable effect in 1999, but did have a strong interaction effect in 2004. Whether she could count on her husband in times when she 'inevitably needed help because of her own or another family member's sickness or accident' did not have an effect on distress for homemaker women, but did have a strong effect for the regularly-employed: a husband's emergency assistance was associated with lower distress in regularly-employed women.

With regard to this interaction effect, we should first check if the meaning of 'emergency assistance' is the same between the regularly-employed and homemakers. In the case of homemakers, wives seem to assume that they will cope with the problem primarily and expect their husbands to provide supplementary assistance. Regularly-employed women, on the other hand, seem to expect their husbands to substitute for their role at times when their children are ill—in concrete terms, to be absent from work or return home from work early, and to do nursing or child-care.

These results suggest that, rather than participating in daily household work or child-rearing, dealing with an emergency is a more serious problem for a double-earner couple. Although strict comparison is difficult because the wording of items was not identical in 1999 and 2004, it seems reasonable to see one reason for the change as being that wives began to expect their husbands to participate in such activities (providing emergency assistance), and another reason as that wives who choose to work as regular employees, regardless of kin support, have been increasing. As seen previously, the things to be expected of husbands are gradually enlarging as a result of social policy aimed toward creating a so-called 'gender-equal society,' and it may turn out that a husband's cooperation with his wife has a great effect on his wife's well-being.

The effect of parents

With regard to parental support, we could not find remarkable effects at both points. However, as NFRJ has only a few items assessing daily support from parents, it might be possible that the results were caused by poor measurement. As the availability of parental support in an emergency is high for both homemakers and the regularly-employed, the functions of these relationships are undoubtedly still important. Logically, the more the importance of husband's role increases, the less dependency on kin decreases, so it may be possible that the role of kin has been more greatly reduced than ever, but this is difficult to ascertain. We have to confirm this issue by using a data set which has more detailed information about the kin relationship.

The effect of a husband's expressive support

The effect of a husband's expressive support has already been mentioned in previous studies. The strong effect of a husband's expressive support, rather than his participation in household work or child-rearing, means that his 'taking care of a wife who herself is a carer' has much more importance than 'sharing care.' As the degree of this effect was equal for both homemakers and the regularly-employed, this effect was not peculiar to regularly-employed women. After all, the main person in charge of household work and child-rearing has been the wife, regardless of whether she is employed, and it may turn out that we observed such a traditional gendered division of labour both in 1999 and in 2004.

From kin to husband: a change in the gendered division of labour?

In a society operating under the strict gendered division of labour, it is well known that a husband's low participation in household work does not cause dissatisfaction for wives (Greenstein 1996; Fuwa 2004; Fuwa and Tsutsui 2006). In general, a weakened gendered division of labour is supposed to cause a wife's dissatisfaction with her husband's low participation in household work, and to prompt her to request her husband to participate (Suemori 1999).

Previous studies in Japan had found that Japanese double-earner families had depended much on kin for household work and child-rearing (Inaba 1999b). The interaction effect of a husband's participation in child-rearing found in this current study may show a transitional change in child-rearing practices, from sharing within intergenerational relationships to sharing within the marital relationship. At least, wives have begun to ask their husbands to share child-rearing, so if that request is not fulfilled, wives seem to experience psychological dissatisfaction.

These processes of change can be considered as one example of the typical structural-change process which occur in social systems, in that a social norm has been weakened, dissatisfaction has become manifest among people of relatively worse-off status, and questioning about old social structures has arisen. Moreover, we can predict that if the conditions that promote husbands' participation in child-rearing—a reduction in working hours, for example—are fulfilled, then male participation will dramatically increase.

Conclusion

Regular employment had much psychological advantage for women in the 1999 data, but no hypothesis could explain this mechanism. Low psychological distress among regularly-employed women could not be explained by a husband's participation in household work, availability of emergency assistance, availability of kin support, or a husband's expressive support. On this point, we have much work to do in terms of analysis of the 1999 data. Conversely, in the 2004 data, if a husband participates in child-rearing or has substitutability in emergencies, a wife's regular employment is associated with low distress for her. As we have seen, a husband's role for an employed wife becomes larger, and how a husband reacts to his wife seems to have much relation with a wife's psychological state. What does this mean?

Though the wife's or husband's parents had more substitutability than husbands, what affected a wife's psychological distress was her husband's emergency assistance. On this point, we should conclude that husbands have been expected by their wives to substitute for the latter's role in an emergency. It is fully possible that such changes have occurred as a result of gender-equalisation policies. Thus, it may be said that the gendered division of labour among couples or families has been gradually changing.

Moreover, though we usually conceptualise role-overload only within the daily role structure, it may be better to think that typical role-overload manifests when an unusual event has occurred. Previous mental-health research has tended to set its focus on the daily role structure, but substitutability in non-daily situations, namely role-overload in a non-daily role, also should be worth examining. From this point of view, we dare to assert that the significance of nursing leave is huge. If husbands can flexibly take nursing leave when their child or wife is sick, then the well-being of regularly-employed women will improve. One could go so far as to say that, rather than their husbands' participation in household work or child-rearing, it is of greater worth to women if those husbands can take leave in an emergency.

One of the institutions which is responding to this problem, as well as nursing leave, is the provision of care services for ill children (*byōji hoiku*: day-care centres for temporarily-unwell children). However, it is natural to think that children would experience much anxiety and stress if they were left in an unfamiliar day-care centre. Of course, there are cases in which parents cannot help but use such care services for their sick children, but it would also be necessary to prepare for such circumstances so that a familiar person could take care of the children in an accustomed environment.

In present-day Japan (after April 2005), nursing leave has become a formal institution that allows parents to take up to five days' (unpaid) leave per year—apart from their paid vacation leave—when their pre-schooler children become sick or injured. However, it seems difficult to cope with a limit of only five days a year when children are pre-schoolers, especially if they are babies or infants. At least, we can say that enhancing nursing leave is the imperative task from the point of view of balancing child-care and employment, and the creation of a climate conducive to the taking of nursing leave is of much importance.

Limitations of this study

Though this study used two representative data sets, both sample sizes of regularly-employed women with pre-schoolers were only small, so the possibility of Type II error cannot be ruled out.[3] Additionally, as the items corresponding to this study were limited, we merely conducted verification of the hypotheses within a limited range. It will be necessary to conduct the same analyses using other data sets, and to cumulate the findings further.

3 Gender and Leadership Effectiveness in the Workplace

Kiriko Sakata

According to the 2005 *Rōdōryoku chōsa* (Labour force survey) published by the Statistics Bureau of the Japanese government's Ministry of Internal Affairs and Communications (Sōmushō Tōkei-kyoku), the proportion of the total employed population occupied by females in Japan had reached 41.3 per cent in 2005. This figure represents a 5.4-point rise over that of 1985, when the Equal Employment Opportunity Law (EEOL) was formulated. Examination of the 2005 ratio of females by occupation reveals that clerical workers accounted for the highest proportion, at 59.9 per cent, with employees in security or service jobs next, at 56.3 per cent, followed by workers in professional or skilled occupations, at 47.6 per cent. On the other hand, while the female share of such occupations was high, the ratio of women in managerial positions overall was extremely small even in 2005, at only 9.6 per cent, and the proportion of females declined in inverse proportion to the seniority of the position, as 10.4 per cent of sub-section chiefs, 5.1 per cent of section chiefs, but only 2.8 per cent of division heads or higher-ranking officers were female (Nijūisseiki Shokugyō Zaidan 2006a). Thus, though the ratio of women in employment has risen, the proportion of females in managerial positions remains low. This dearth of female executives throws up a variety of hurdles for women in management jobs and, at the same time, impresses upon young female employees who have just begun their work career that it is difficult for women to be promoted to managerial positions, and this has become a factor prompting them to abandon the idea of becoming a core member of their organisation. Given the current situation in Japan, one must admit that it is extremely hard for women to develop a work career which includes a managerial occupation in its scope.

What might be the factors that give rise to this difficulty? According to a survey conducted in 2005 by the Japan Institute of Workers' Evolution (Nijūisseiki Shokugyō Zaidan), which targeted officers in charge of personnel or human resources in First- or

Second-section listed companies in Tokyo, Osaka and Nagoya, the premier reason for hindering the utilisation and recruitment of women is 'The large number quitting jobs on the momentum of childbirth or child-rearing' (42.8 per cent), and the greatest cause for this can be assumed to be the incomplete preparation of an environment—exemplified by a lack of childcare facilities—which would enable women to raise their children without quitting their jobs during child-bearing and child-raising periods. If one looks at the reasons given by firms with no increase in the ratio of female managers, however, the next most common justification after: 'The majority of women lacks work experience' (57.0 per cent) is: 'They have insufficient decision-making, planning and negotiation powers' (34.7 per cent), which attributes the problem to deficiencies in women's personal ability; and this greatly exceeds attribution to situational factors such as: 'Performance appraisal works more to male than to female advantage' (8.8 per cent) (Nijūisseiki Shokugyō Zaidan 2006b). Such perceptions vis-à-vis women's capacity suggest that even if issues to do with women's family responsibilities such as childbirth and child-raising have been resolved, there still remain factors which make it difficult for women to exercise leadership capabilities in the workplace.

In this chapter, I focus upon the workplace in my examination of the mechanism by which female leadership effectiveness is lowered (or heightened) in comparison to that of males. In this realm, research has been carried out either by the macro approach, which concentrates mainly upon socio-constructive or organisational factors, or the micro approach, which focuses upon interpersonal cognition and interpersonal transaction processes between leaders and followers, and the views of the majority of researchers already coincide on several points. On the basis of these congruent findings, I endeavour in this chapter to construct a hypothetical model relating to the generation of gender differences in leaders' effectiveness, by showing how organisational/group-level and individual-level factors which govern gender differences in leadership effectiveness impact upon interpersonal cognition and interpersonal transaction between leaders and followers. While this study concentrates upon a limited society, namely a work organisation, it aims to offer a framework for understanding how women's influence is restricted or promoted by various social and psychological factors, in the pursuance of a leadership role which is one of the roles most uncongenial with the traditional female role.

Moreover, though a number of surveys have been carried out in Japan on the actual state of women's awareness of what constitutes a management position, or on employees' and employers' awareness as to the recruitment of female managers, et cetera, there has been very little research conducted from a social psychological perspective, in comparison with the West. For that reason, a major part of the rationale employed in the establishment of the hypothesis in this chapter needs to rely upon previous Western studies. I do, however, base my exploration of the possibility of the proposed hypothetical model being supported in Japan on the scant amount of existing Japanese research. In light of the current situation of incongruence between leadership roles and women's roles, and the presence of a 'glass ceiling,' there is considered to be no fundamental difference between Japan and the West in terms of the conditions surrounding female leaders, but I will add a few consideration at the end of this chapter in regard to issues unique to Japan which diverge from those of the West.

Gender, leadership behaviour and leadership effectiveness

The leadership effectiveness indicators which have been employed in conventional leadership studies are diverse, and examples which could be cited include group productivity, absenteeism and laziness, morale and motivation, satisfaction towards work and leaders, followers' self-concept and identity, a sense of organisational belongingness, stress and mental health, and so on. The focus of gender-related leadership research has mainly been subjective indicators based upon assessments by subordinates, colleagues, bosses or leaders themselves, such as the evaluation of satisfaction towards leaders or leadership performance appraisal (Eagly, Karau and Makhijani 1995). Consequently, most of the previous research associated with leaders and leadership effectiveness must be interpreted as having been concerned with effectiveness indicators such as those expressing endorsement of leaders or acceptance of leaders' influence, rather than effectiveness indicators such as those which directly reflect the objective productivity of the work-group.

It goes without saying that the major factor affecting leadership effectiveness is the leadership behaviour and influence tactics of leaders. The situation in which research examining leadership behaviour and influence tactics in relation to gender has focused solely upon comparatively limited types of behaviour is similar to that mentioned in the case with leadership effectiveness indicators. In the realm of leadership studies in recent years, various frameworks have been proposed, such as political leadership (Ammeter, Douglas, Gardner, Hochwarter and Ferris 2002; Treadway, Hochwarter, Ferris, Kacmar, Douglas, Ammeter and Buckley 2004); Leader–Member Exchange (LMX) theory, which concentrates upon reciprocal exchange relationships between leaders and members (Graen and Uhl-Bien 1995); and social-constructivist leadership studies which focus upon followers' cognition (Meindl 1995; van Knippenberg, van Knippenberg, De Cremer and Hogg 2005), but the majority of research which incorporates the perspective of gender focuses upon task-oriented versus relationship-oriented behaviour or democratic versus autocratic management styles (Eagly and Johnson 1990; Hollander and Yoder 1980), while recently there have been several studies which concentrate upon transformational versus transactional leadership behaviour (Eagly, Johannesen-Schmidt and van Engen 2003). These kinds of leadership behaviour are thought to have been frequently taken up because they constitute the framework for the most fundamental leadership behaviour—each, at the same time, being classifiable from a gender-stereotypical viewpoint into feminine or masculine behaviour.

On the dimension of task-oriented versus relationship-oriented behaviour, it is shown by many studies (e.g., Blake and Mouton 1964; House and Dessler 1974; Misumi 1985) that leadership effectiveness is highest in terms of both objective and subjective indicators in leaders who rate highly on both behavioural frequencies rather than on one or the other, and who are able to utilise both types of behaviour selectively as the occasion demands. It is clear, however, that in leaderless groups, people who are viewed as leaders by group members when tasks are to be carried out are those who display task-oriented behaviour rather than relationship-oriented behaviour (Lockheed and Hall 1976). This is thought to be due to people's prototypical image of the leadership role being more firmly tied to task-oriented behaviour (Lord and Maher 1991). In other words, fundamentally, leaders who exhibit a high level of both task-oriented and relationship-oriented behaviour are the most effective, but it can be appreciated that task-oriented behaviour is essential for them to be endorsed as legitimate leaders by their followers. On the other hand, in terms of democratic versus autocratic management style, at least in regard to subjective effectiveness indicators such as followers' satisfaction, it is clear that democratic leaders show higher leadership effectiveness than autocratic leaders (Foels, Driskell, Mullen and Salas 2000; Gastil 1994). Moreover, while these types of leadership behaviour include some examples in which leadership effectiveness changes according to the situation in which the group is placed (e.g., Fiedler 1967; House and Dessler 1974), the number of studies relating to gender and leadership whose scope encompasses such regulating factors is exceptionally small.

Considering the above current situation, one should probably regard most previous research on gender and leadership behaviour, as well as on leadership effectiveness, as being limited to that which focuses upon extremely basic elements of the leadership process. Accordingly, this chapter will also attempt to establish a hypothetical model centring upon these basic elements.

Theories on gender differences in leadership effectiveness

Most studies relating to gender and leadership effectiveness have been conducted from the standpoint of expectation-states theory (Berger, Fisek, Norman and Zelditch 1977; Berger, Wagner and Zelditch 1985) or social-role theory (Eagly 1987).

According to expectation-states theory, members of a task-executing group will search for a member who appears likely to make a large contribution to the attainment of their goal, and will voluntarily accept the influence of the member who is thus regarded. In circumstances where there is information pertaining to the extent to which each member possesses skills of direct relevance to the attainment of the goal or task, this will comprise the status characteristics which create performance expectations. Characteristics such as these which directly relate to goal-attainment skills are called specific-status characteristics. When such direct status information is not available, however, diffuse-status characteristics (namely, general characteristics which have a correlation with social status and ability, such as gender, race or education) which are external to the organisation or group (that is, society) create performance expectations. Group members regard people with high status in terms of diffuse-status characteristics as possessing greater task-execution capability than do people with low status. Group members expect that high-status people will demonstrate their competence in a self-confident manner which will assert their status, but low-status people are likely to have their task contribution ignored or rejected, as they are not expected to behave in such a way (Ridgeway 2001). In other words, low-status people lack the legitimacy necessary for acting as leaders or exerting their influence. According to expectation-states theory, gender is one of the diffuse-status characteristics, and if a category called gender is salient among the numerous diffuse-status characteristics, then gender will create performance expectations. In this case, as men are socially of higher status than women, even if the group task be gender-neutral in terms of gender stereotypes, it can be predicted that men will wield greater influence than women, and have higher leadership effectiveness.

Meanwhile, in social-role theory, it is assumed that gender differences in behaviour and influence will arise more from expectations and norms based on the social roles of males and females than from status differences of women and men in society. The essence of female and male roles is communion or agency, respectively (Bakan 1966). As people generally think that agency is necessary for success as a leader, it is shown from numerous studies that the leadership role and the male role are congruent, but the leadership role and female role are not (e.g., Schein 1973, 1975, 2001). Eagly and Karau (2002) argue that this incongruity between the leadership role and the female role gives rise to the following two types of bias: (a) as leadership ability is stereotypically more a male than a female attribute, assessment of women's leadership ability becomes more negative than that of males; and (b) as leadership behaviour is perceived as less desirable for females than for males, assessment of actual female leadership behaviour becomes negative. From these biases, it can be predicted that female leaders will tend generally to experience more difficulties than male leaders. In social-role theory, however, as leadership roles such as those in which women are thought to have comparatively greater interest and performance capability (educational leadership, for example) have congeniality with females, one predicts that female leaders will sometimes outrank male leaders in effectiveness, without being the target of strong bias (Carli 2001; Eagly et al. 1995; Eagly, Makhijani and Klonsky 1992).

These two theories can be considered complementary rather than contrary in their explanation of gender difference in leadership effectiveness. Seldom are dissident predictions educed from these two theories in relation to gender differences in leadership processes (one exception being Berdahl 1996). As I later discuss, predictions from both theories are generally supported empirically. On occasions when the object of consideration is the process in which interaction between organisational or group factors and individual factors influences gender differences in leadership effectiveness by way of influence upon interpersonal cognition and interpersonal transaction, these two theoretical frameworks will again be made the base.

Organisational and group determinants of differences

The gender congeniality of tasks or leadership roles and the gender-composition ratio of groups can be cited as examples of organisational and group factors which have been noted as factors determining the effectiveness of female and male leaders.

Eagly et al. (1995) conducted meta-analysis of ninety-six cases of empirical research relating to gender differences in leadership effectiveness, and found that the effectiveness of female and male leaders differed according to the gender congeniality of leadership roles. The gender congeniality of leadership roles refers to the extent to which men and women are interested in those roles and have the ability to perform them, as well as the degree to which gender-stereotypical characteristics are deemed necessary in order to carry out those roles. The congeniality of tasks is a concept which indicates whether group tasks are considered to be stereotypically oriented towards males or females (Carbonell 1984; Hollander and Yoder 1980), and is thought to be a concept with a strong association with the gender congeniality of leadership roles. In the meta-analysis conducted by Eagly et al. (1995), it was shown that the more leadership roles require interpersonal abilities such as cooperation with others, the more effective female leaders will be, while male leaders are the more effective the greater the requirement is for the ability to instruct and control others. Similarly, in military organisations, it has also been found that male leaders are clearly the more effective (Eagly et al. 1995), which suggests that male leaders are more effective than female leaders in organisations which perform exceedingly masculine-type tasks or in those where males are numerically superior. As for the gender-composition ratio of groups, it has been shown that male leaders are more effective than female leaders the more males there are among subordinates (Eagly et al. 1995), and that women receive lower assessments than men in performance appraisals the smaller the proportion of females in the group becomes (Sackett, DuBois and Noe 1991).

By what processes might the gender-congeniality of tasks or leadership roles and the gender-composition ratio of groups give rise to gender differences in leadership effectiveness? The following two processes are suggested from previous research. The first is the possibility that female leaders' effectiveness declines in terms of subjective performance-appraisal and motivation indicators, in particular, due to the presence of evaluative bias vis-à-vis women, even if female leaders and male leaders have actually exhibited equally effective leadership behaviour. The second is the possibility that female leaders actually cease to exercise leadership behaviour in groups where the leadership role is congenial to males or males have numerical superiority.

The number of studies suggesting the first process is large. Eagly et al. (1992), who carried out meta-analysis of research which manipulated only the gender of leaders which controlled their leadership behaviour and characteristics, and had participants evaluate leaders' abilities and their satisfaction towards leaders, have found that when female leaders employed a masculine leadership style (an autocratic style, for example), they received a more negative evaluation than did male leaders, though no gender difference could be confirmed in the case of a feminine leadership style, and male assessors assigned a lower evaluation to female leaders than to male leaders. Moreover, Sackett et al. (1991) have found that even if researchers controlled such factors as cognitive ability test scores and experience in organisations, women received lower performance appraisals than men the smaller the proportion of females became, and male tokens did not receive as low an appraisal as in the case of female tokens. These findings suggest that in cases where women exercise male-congenial leadership behaviour or when they are in workplaces where males are in the majority, women receive lower performance appraisals than men, even if there is no disparity in terms of ability.

This evaluative bias which arises in male-congenial tasks and leadership roles can be explained by the previously-mentioned two theories—in other words, by both expectation-states theory and social-role theory. In expectation-states theory, even if the group be one engaged in tasks which are neutral in terms of gender-congeniality, it is considered that women's legitimacy as leaders is perceived to be low because the lowness of their status in society is seen as uncongenial with the high-status role of leader. Even if a low-status woman were to act self-confidently and assertively, in a manner befitting a person of high status, such behaviour would be unlikely to be tolerated because group members would not expect such conduct from a person of low status (Ridgeway and Berger 1986; Yoder 2001). According to Ridgeway (2001), this tendency is even more intensified in groups engaged in male-congenial tasks. This is because, in addition to the fact that women are of lower status than men in terms of diffuse-status characteristics, women are also perceived as being inferior to men in terms of specific-status characteristics directly relating to tasks in groups engaging in male-congenial tasks. When tasks are female-congenial, even if women are inferior to men in terms of diffuse-status characteristics, there is potential for women to be viewed as being of higher status than men, and thus no difference is likely to be seen in the performance appraisals of female and male leaders, respectively. In social-role theory, on the other hand, as the incongruence between women's gender role and leadership role becomes even greater in cases where the leadership role is male-congenial, female leaders have their abilities rated even lower in comparison to cases where the leadership role is female-congenial or neutral (Carli 2001; Eagly et al. 1995; Eagly and Karau 2002).

In the second process, there seem to be multiple patterns. One involves the possibility that, in cases where tasks or leadership roles are male-congenial, female leaders will find it more difficult to engage in task-oriented behaviour. Eagly and Johnson (1990), who conducted meta-analysis of the various studies relating to gender differences in leadership behaviour, have found that both men and women behave in a task-oriented manner when they are in roles stereotypically congenial to their own gender. This tendency has also been reported in other research (e.g., Hollander and Yoder 1980). Conversely, it is thought that people find it more difficult to engage in task-oriented behaviour when they are in roles uncongenial to their own gender. Eagly and Johnson (1990) have explained this result from the standpoint of social-role theory.

In groups with a male majority, on the other hand, it is also pointed out that it is difficult for female leaders to behave in a relationship-oriented or democratic manner. Eagly and Johnson (1990) showed that the tendency for women to exhibit gender-stereotypical behaviour (namely, a relationship-oriented and democratic style) grows weaker in inverse proportion to the ratio of males among the group under evaluation. In this connection, as a result of comparing managerial positions in female-dominant organisations with organisations where males are numerically superior (in this case, organisations in which the proportion of women accounts for less than fifteen per cent, both within the organisation as a whole and at the managerial level), Gardiner and Tiggemann (1999) have found that though women in managerial positions in a female-dominant organisation behave in a more relationship-oriented manner than do its male managers, female managers in a male-dominated organisation act in a more task-oriented way than its men who occupy executive positions. Furthermore, though the mental health of female managers in male-dominant organisations worsens the more they adopt a relationship-oriented style, no link was acknowledged between leadership style and mental health in female-dominant organisations. Gardiner and Tiggemann (1999) interpret this result as meaning that female leaders in a male-dominant organisation perhaps tend to repress their relationship-oriented behaviour and adopt a task-oriented style because they would become gender-stereotyped and be less likely to be seen as able leaders if they displayed a feminine leadership style (a relationship-oriented style, for example).

In actual organisations, in the same way that men are supposed to be in the majority when tasks are male-congenial, it will probably often happen that the gender-congeniality of tasks or leadership roles will show a strong association with male numerical superiority. If this be true, then, on the one hand, in organisations where tasks and leadership roles are male-congenial and males have a numerical advantage (such organisations will hereafter be called male-dominant organisations), female leaders will find themselves in a situation where it is difficult for them fundamentally to adopt a task-oriented style because the tasks and leadership roles are not congruent with their own gender, but there is an accompanying risk of relationship-oriented or democratic behaviour being gender-stereotyped, and so the women have no choice but to repress such behaviour, after all. This not only signifies the powerful dilemma in which female leaders find themselves, but also can be thought to mean that female leaders' behaviour will tend to become negative, on the whole. If this interpretation be correct, then women in male-dominant organisations have the potential to reduce their own leadership effectiveness as measured by objective indicators, through the increasing difficulty they experience in exercising effective leadership behaviour. What is more, if one applies the aforementioned considerations relating to evaluative bias, it can be seen that even if women adopt a strongly task-oriented style (taken to be behaviour which is expected of high-status persons or male-congenial behaviour) in order to avoid being gender-stereotyped in a male-dominant organisation, they will also end up reducing their leadership effectiveness in terms of subjective indicators because they undermine status-related or gender-role expectations.

Another pattern belonging to the second process is the potential for the expectation that female leaders will not be effective to become self-fulfilling, by means of the stereotype threat effect. Stereotype threat refers to the phenomenon that when a negative stereotype about the ability of a social group in a particular task domain becomes salient, individual group members become concerned that their performance may confirm the validity of the negative stereotype. It has been made clear that stereotype threat actually does degrade the task performance of the group members (Steele and Aronson 1995). The task-performance degradation phenomenon triggered by stereotype threat has been confirmed thus far in areas such as women's mathematics performance (Spencer, Steele and Quinn 1999), African-Americans' intellectual test performance (Steele and Aronson 1995) and whites' athletic performance (Stone, Lynch, Sjomeling and Darley 1999). Though stereotype threat research into women's leadership ability is still scant, it has been suggested that women's leadership aspirations do actually decline in contexts of the activation of gender stereotypes (Davies, Spencer and Steele 2005).

It has thus been shown that the leadership effectiveness of female leaders in male-dominant groups or organisations declines in comparison to that of male leaders because of evaluative bias, or because female leaders' behaviour is in actual fact restricted. By contrast, differing predictions can be drawn from expectation-states theory and social-role theory, respectively, as to whether female leaders are more effective than male leaders in cases where the leadership role is female-congenial or women are in the majority. In regard to female-dominant groups or organisations, though women's status will be high in terms of task-contribution according to the viewpoint of expectation-states theory, it is predicted that women will seldom surpass male leaders' effectiveness, as men are of higher status in terms of diffuse-status characteristics. According to social-role theory, on the other hand, as the female role coincides with the leadership role, the leadership of female leaders is capable of surpassing that of male leaders. The meta-analytical results of Eagly et al. (1995) support the predictions of social-role theory.

Individual factors

As I have already stated, it is suggested that male dominance in groups or organisations lowers the objective and subjective effectiveness of female leaders more than that of male leaders by functioning to limit the range of activities allowed to female leaders. However, leaders' ability deftly to overcome such a difficult situation and exercise effective leadership probably differs according to individual factors of the leaders themselves. From various studies pertaining to individual characteristics of leaders themselves, gender identity, self-monitoring and social skills can be cited as principal factors associated with leadership effectiveness. It is suggested that rather than directly determining leadership effectiveness, leaders' individual characteristics tend more to exert an indirect influence upon it, mediated by their impact upon leadership behaviour.

In regard to gender identity, the Bem Sex Role Inventory (BSRI) (Bem 1974) is often utilised, people who ascribe characteristics of both femininity (or communion) and masculinity (or agency) to themselves to a high degree frequently being classified as androgynous types; people high on femininity and low on masculinity as feminine types; people low on femininity and high on masculinity as masculine types; and people low on both scores as undifferentiated types. It is consistently shown from previous research that a leader's degree of masculinity is associated with the extent to which he or she is perceived as a leader by group members, regardless of leaders' gender (Fagenson 1990; Goktepe and Schneier 1989; Hall, Workman and Marchioro 1998; Kent and Moss 1994; Kolb 1997). If one considers that the masculinity scale in BSRI is made up of items which express agency or instrumentality, and that people who positively display task-related behaviour tend to be perceived as leaders by group members, then it probably can be deduced that people with a high masculinity score will exhibit positive task-related behaviour, and thus become all the more likely to be perceived by group members as leaders.

On the other hand, there are also some studies which have shown that androgynous types also tend to be perceived as leaders (Kent and Moss 1994; Hall et al. 1998). The work of Hall et al. (1998), in particular, is of deep interest due to its indication that a positive correlation between androgyny and perceived leadership is seen only among females in groups which perform masculine tasks (manufacturing games). As it has also been shown that, basically, both task-oriented and relationship-oriented behaviour are necessary for effective leadership (Blake and Mouton 1964; House and Dessler 1974; Misumi 1985); and leaders who can alter their behaviour in a flexible manner as the need arises are effective (Hooijberg 1996); and, as androgynous people are considered capable of flexibly adjusting their behaviour to suit the situation (Bem 1974), an androgynous identity is thought to enhance leadership effectiveness because it is tied to a broad repertoire of leadership behaviour and the skill flexibly to select appropriate action from it (Hall et al. 1998). Moreover, considered from the perspective of social-role theory, leaders who can demonstrate communal behaviour as the occasion demands will probably be more positively evaluated than those showing only agentic behaviour which does not coincide with their gender role, especially in the case of women. As Hall et al. (1998) show, this ability is thought to be particularly advantageous to female leaders in groups which perform male-congenial tasks.

Even given the same individual factors associated with the flexibility of leadership behaviour, the effects of self-monitoring are complex. Self-monitoring (hereafter referred to as SM) is defined as the observation and socially-appropriate regulation of one's own behaviour and self-presentation, based on situational cues and the behaviour of others (Snyder 1974; 1979). It is suggested that, in leaderless small groups, high-SM members are generally the most likely to emerge as leaders (Dobbins, Long, Dedrick and Clemons 1990; Eby, Cader and Noble 2003), which is attributed to high-SM people's ability to engage in flexible behaviour (Zaccaro, Foti and Kenny 1991). The work of Hall et al. (1998)—one of the few studies to have examined the effects of leaders' SM from the perspective of gender—shows that the connection between SM and leadership perception by group members is stronger in males than in females. Furthermore, in Becker, Ayman and Korabik (2002), incongruence between leaders' self-perception and followers' perception vis-à-vis the leaders' behaviour was shown to be greater for high-SM females than for low-SM females in industrial organisations, as a result of comparing occupiers of managerial positions in industrial organisations with those in educational organisations. As incongruence between leaders' self-perception and followers' perception indicates a lack of recognition of leaders' behaviour on the part of followers, this is thought to be linked with low leadership effectiveness. Moreover, male norms such as competition and agency are considered to be predominant in industrial organisations, and female norms such as nurturance and communion to be predominant in educational organisations. These results thus suggest that high-SM females in managerial positions in organisations which have masculine norms will have lower leadership effectiveness than low-SM female managers.

Becker et al. (2002) offer the following interpretation of why a high-SM tendency, which is generally expected to work to the advantage of leadership effectiveness, should have the opposite result in the case of female leaders in organisations with masculine norms. Incongruence between leaders' self-perception and followers' perception relating to leaders' behaviour is ascribable to cognitive differences, namely that while actors' self-perception is strongly influenced by situational cues and anticipated role-behaviour, observers' perception is not readily influenced by social conditions, because their attention is drawn to actors' salient traits (Jones and Nisbett 1972). The role of manager is probably salient for actors (leaders), and actors' gender is probably salient for observers (followers). Though high-SM women in managerial positions seek to engage in behaviour aligned with the surrounding masculine norms (and thus try to conduct themselves in a task-oriented or autocratic manner), as leaders' characteristic (namely, their being female) constitutes the most salient cue for perceivers in such an organisation, they perceive female leaders' behaviour as being feminine. This causes greater incongruence between leaders' and followers' perception. As the sample size is small in the research of Becker et al. (2002), prudence is required in interpreting its results, but they are very interesting in that they show there can be a tendency for high-SM female leaders to attempt to fit masculine norms, rather than to try to respond to followers' expectations. In the case of male leaders, no incongruence between leaders' and followers' perception is likely to arise because expectations from followers and the requirements of masculine norms are congruent, regardless of to whichever of these the leaders accommodate themselves. Given that women in numerically male-dominant organisations already face a serious dilemma, there is a risk that high-SM women will become trapped in an even greater dilemma because they try harder than low-SM women to respond to the demands of each situation. When one considers the findings from these two studies, one must conclude that there is still ambiguity as to whether a high SM tendency brings any benefit to female leaders.

As for social skills, their effect is suggested by various studies which have explored methods for making female leadership effective.

As I have already stated, female leaders are especially likely to face difficulties in male-dominant organisations, but it has been pointed out that group-oriented behaviour, respect for others and a sense of humour (Yoder 2001), as well as mindfulness (Kawakami, White and Langer 2000) on the part of female leaders themselves is necessary to enhance those leaders' effectiveness in such a masculine context. Yoder (2001) indicates that, from the standpoint of expectation-states theory, it is necessary to raise women's status through the legitimisation by authority figures of female leaders' abilities in masculine contexts where the lowness of women's status is most readily salient, but there is also a simultaneous need for women themselves to behave prudently in order not to violate surrounding expectations vis-à-vis people of low status, even while demonstrating their own high level of competence. In concrete terms, this shows that women's exhibiting group rather than individual orientation—meaning working for the sake of the group—and not assertively flaunting their own abilities, but rather demonstrating them with a little humour while having respect for others, enhances female leaders' effectiveness. From a social-role theory perspective, also, these types of behaviour have the potential to ameliorate the surrounding perception that female leaders violate gender roles, as each type of behaviour is communal—in other words, female-congenial. The 'mindfulness' pointed out by Kawakami et al. (2000) refers not to engaging in by-the-book masculine leadership-role behaviour, but to the skill of using one's own mind to conceive behaviour appropriate to each occasion, and expressing it. Even if female leaders do employ masculine leadership behaviour (in this case, cold-hearted behaviour), the masculine behaviour of 'mindful' leaders will make those leaders less likely to be viewed as uncongenial than that of 'mindless' leaders, and the former will be perceived to be good leaders who have 'genuineness' (Kawakami et al. 2000). Whether such behaviour as group-orientation, respect for others, humour or mindfulness will be possible is thought to depend on actors' level of social skills. The three basic elements of social skills are considered to be accurately reading information from others (decoding), accurately conveying one's own intention in response to the first (encoding), and regulating one's own communicative behaviour (regulation) (Riggio 1986). A high level of such social skills is probably essential for enhancing female leaders' effectiveness in masculine contexts.

In short, this implies that gender identity and social skills are individual traits which can be thought to be associated with gender differences in leadership effectiveness. These two traits are both factors involved in allowing breadth and flexibility to exist in the repertoire of leadership behaviour. Androgynous gender identity has the potential to heighten women's leadership effectiveness by enabling flexible behaviour, especially in cases where masculine tasks are to be executed. Especially in male-dominant organisations or groups, social skills are also thought to be useful in enhancing leadership effectiveness through their amelioration of surrounding perceptions that female leaders are encroaching upon the roles of low-status persons or gender roles, even while demonstrating their leadership competence. These individual traits and organisational and group factors are considered to have an interactional influence upon gender differences in leadership effectiveness.

The hypothetical model

Based on the above discussion, the mechanism by which gender differences in leadership effectiveness emerge is represented in Figure 3.1. First, the male dominance of the organisation or group makes gender salient itself, and facilitates the activation of gender stereotypes (Arrow *a*). If we think in terms of the social-role theory framework, the incongruence between leadership roles and gender roles in relation to female leaders will expand due to the activation of gender stereotypes, and that will lower female leaders' effectiveness (Arrow *b*). If, on the other hand, we think in terms of the expectation-states theory framework, then followers will position female leaders as low-status persons and perceive their legitimacy as leaders to be low, due to focus being directed at gender as a diffuse-status characteristic (Arrow *c*). This works towards lowering evaluation and satisfaction towards female leaders, as well as reducing their effectiveness by spawning resistance to their influence (Arrow *d*). In the case of male leaders, as congruence between leadership roles and gender roles will be enhanced, this series of processes, *a*, *b*, *c* and *d*, probably functions to heighten both the legitimacy of male leaders and their leadership effectiveness.

On the other hand, the male dominance in organisations or groups sometimes actually regulates leaders' behaviour (Arrow *e*). This Arrow *e* means that while the male-congeniality of tasks makes it difficult for female leaders to behave in a task-oriented manner, the numerical superiority of males also suppresses female leaders' relationship-oriented behaviour at the same time. As this leads,

Figure 3.1: The hypothetical model of gender-difference in leadership effectiveness

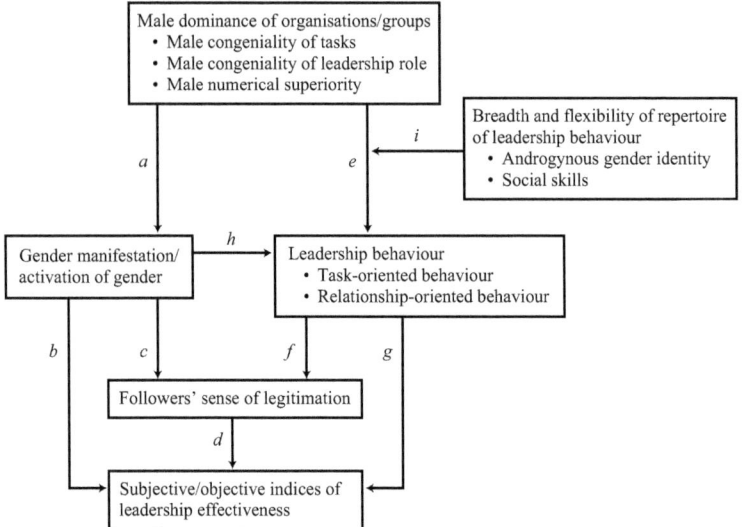

the numerical superiority of males also suppresses female leaders' relationship-oriented behaviour at the same time. As this leads to effective leadership becoming impossible to exercise, harmful effects would be exerted upon objective leadership-effectiveness indicators (Arrow g). Even should female leaders display strong task-orientation adapted to male behavioural norms, such behaviour would not be expected of women as persons of low status, and this would also violate gender norms, so women ultimately would be seen to be lacking in legitimacy (Arrow f), and this would reduce their leadership effectiveness (Arrow d). Moreover, through the activation of gender stereotypes, female leaders would be more likely to experience stereotype threat, and potentially would become unable to engage in effective behaviour (Arrow h). In cases where the leadership behaviour repertoire of female leaders was broad and richly flexible, because such women would be able to conduct themselves in a way so as not to violate gender norms or the norms of low-status persons even while displaying their competence as leaders, and would be able to flexibly to utilise different task-orientations or relationship-orientations according to the circumstances, they would be able to mitigate the adverse impact of male dominance in the organisation or group (Arrow i). As for male leaders, male dominance in the organisation or group does not particularly restrict leadership behaviour (Arrow e), and therefore probably would not have a negative influence upon leadership effectiveness (Arrows f, g, d).

Examination of Japanese theoretical models

Most previous research relating to leadership effectiveness has been carried out in the United States and Western Europe. Gender roles in Japanese society, however, are far more traditional than those in Western countries. According to the International Comparative Survey on Gender Equality (*Danjo kyōdō sankaku shakai ni kansuru kokusai hikaku chōsa*) conducted in 2002 by the Equality Bureau of the Japanese Cabinet Office (Naikakufu Danjo Kyōdō Sankaku-kyoku), 62.8 per cent of U.S. respondents and 49.7 per cent of respondents from the United Kingdom indicated complete or partial agreement with the statement that men were favourably treated in society in general, but this figure soared to 78.4 per cent in Japan. According to a survey conducted by the same bureau in 2004, though the proportion of people in Japan clearly rejecting the gendered division of labour which dictates that 'a husband should work outside the home, while a wife should be a full-time homemaker' has reached nearly half the total (48.9 per cent), an overwhelming proportion of responses indicated that the person actually responsible for household work is the wife (cleaning, 77.6 per cent; meal-preparation, 87.4 per cent; clearing up after meals, 78.9 per cent). In Japan, the status difference between males and females is more pronounced than in the West, and one might safely say that traditional gender roles also stubbornly persist (though such attitudes are in the process of changing). Moreover, as I will later elaborate, it has been empirically demonstrated that in Japan, as in the West, leadership is generally considered to be a role more suited to males than to females (Sakata 2002; Takahashi, Yamaguchi and Ushimaru 1998). Consequently, if one considers these points together with the low ratio of women occupying managerial positions which I mentioned at the beginning of this chapter, expectation-states theory and gender-role theory can be considered amply applicable in Japan, too, as a basis for predicting gender differences in leadership effectiveness.

In regard to male dominance in organisations and groups in Japan, however, a slightly different tendency from that of the West is seen. Takahashi et al. (1998), targeting 395 women who worked in corporate entities, administrative institutions or nursing organisations in Japan, the United States and Australia, conducted a survey on the strength of gender bias (the tendency for females and males to have different types of work duties and status) and gender personality traits suited to work in the organisations to which respondents belonged. The researchers made the following findings, namely that in Japan, it is corporate entities which have the strongest gender bias, followed by administrative institutions, with nursing organisations having the weakest bias—this gender bias tending to weaken somewhat as the numerical ratio of women in the organisation grows. In addition, the degree to which a masculine personality was deemed necessary also dwindled in the order of corporate entities, administrative institutions and nursing organisations, while the degree to which a feminine personality was deemed necessary shrank in reverse order. This result was not affected by the ratio of females in the organisation. In the United States and Australia, on the other hand, gender bias was at about the same level in both corporate entities and administrative institutions, and lowest in nursing organisations. As for the gender personality deemed necessary by institutions, irrespective of the type of organisation, both masculinity and femininity were deemed necessary to a similar degree (in the case of nursing organisations, femininity was deemed more necessary than masculinity). Finally, it was found that in Japan, the U.S. and Australia, too, a masculine personality was significantly more in demand for managerial positions than a feminine one, regardless of the type of institution. These results suggest that leadership roles in corporate entities are most male-congenial, followed by administrative institutions and nursing organisations, and that this tendency is stronger in Japan than in the United States or Australia.

So, might the above-mentioned hypothetical models be supported in Japan? Though there are a few existing studies relating to the effects of organisational or group factors, as I will shortly introduce, there are hardly any to be seen which have examined the interactive effects of leaders' individual factors with organisational or group factors. I will thus explore the independent effects of organisational and group factors here.

Firstly, Sakata and Kurokawa (1992) have examined how the gender-congeniality of tasks differentiates female and male leaders' leadership behaviour and influence strategies, by means of experimental research using university students as participants. With male/female pairs of experimental participants playing the leaders, the researchers set up a scene in which these leaders made a sole follower (a collaborator in the experiment) perform masculine tasks and feminine tasks as efficiently as possible, and while the researchers evaluated the leadership behaviour by means of trained observers and the leaders themselves, they simultaneously evaluated the leadership ability of each leader by means of the followers who were collaborators in the experiment. In order to grant equal expertise and legitimacy to each of the two leaders, the researchers had them experience the tasks in advance, and learn efficient ways of solving the tasks, while at the same time instructing the pairs with emphasis upon the fact that 'both were leaders with the same degree of authority.' As a result, it became clear that for both the frequency of utterance as assessed by the observers and the self-assessed frequency of use of influence strategies, the score was higher in cases where the task was congenial to the leader's gender than when it was uncongenial. A similar result, moreover, was obtained from self-assessment relating to the intentional use of the power of expertise and the power of legitimacy, leadership ability being more highly appraised when the leader's gender was congenial to the task than when it was not. Furthermore, in terms of leadership ability, the main effect of the leader's gender was significant—females' leadership ability receiving a higher evaluation than that of males. These results illustrate that when the gender-congeniality of the task matches that of the leader's gender, both male and female leaders' attempted influence is great, they act positively, they assert expertise and the power of legitimacy, and their effectiveness is actually highly evaluated.

These results are also reproduced in field research on workplaces engaged in gender-neutral or somewhat female-congenial tasks (in other words, departments connected with welfare, health or counselling centres, for example, within administrative bodies) (Sakata and Kurokawa 1993). The study had 430 subordinates (157 females, 273 males) evaluate the leadership behaviour and influence strategies of section chiefs in twenty-six departments in these workplaces. Leadership behaviour was measured using the framework of PM theory (Misumi 1985), which measures leaders' degree of task-performance behaviour (hereafter referred to as P behaviour) and group-maintenance behaviour (hereafter referred to as M behaviour). Planning P behaviour corresponds to initiating-structure factors, pressure P behaviour to production-emphasis, and, similarly, M behaviour to consideration factors of LBDQ (Halpin and Winer 1957). In regard to influence strategies, the following three factors were extracted by factor analysis upon measurement of the usage frequency of nine types of strategy, namely: direct strategies which clearly demonstrate leaders' own power, such as assigning punishments, granting rewards, applying pressure, or asserting expertise; indirect strategies such as explaining rationales, giving suggestions or hints, or turning subordinates' feelings in a positive direction; and powerless strategies including seeking help from subordinates or doing trade-offs.

In the results of analysis, no difference due to the gender of the section chief was acknowledged in relation to the usage frequency of leadership behaviour or influence strategies. It is not surprising even though no gender-based disparity could be acknowledged in the frequency of use of leadership behaviour and strategies when seen from the aspect of the gender-congeniality of tasks or leadership roles. The leadership effectiveness of these types of behaviour, however, did vary according to the gender of the section chief. A clear disparity between male and female section chiefs emerged in the effectiveness of pressure P behaviour as a result of three-way multivariate analysis of variance (MANOVA) of section-chiefs' gender, subordinates' gender, and leadership behaviour, with motivation, the quality of teamwork and effectiveness in group meetings as dependent variables. In other words, in the case of male section chiefs, a positive effect was brought to bear on subordinate groups' teamwork and group meetings when pressure P was strong rather than weak, but in the case of female section chiefs, when pressure P was strong rather than weak, a negative effect was exerted on subordinate groups' teamwork. Moreover, as a result of MANOVA of section-chiefs' gender × subordinates' gender × influence strategies, subordinates' motivation tended to be higher when the frequency of indirect strategy-use by male section chiefs was high rather than low, and when that of female section chiefs was low rather than high. Indirect strategies tend to be considered more female-congenial, while direct strategies tend to be considered more male-congenial, but such effects could not be recognised in relation to direct strategies. What is suggested by this field study is that in cases where tasks and leadership roles are female-congenial, direct strategies by female leaders are just as effective as those of male leaders, but the adoption of female-congenial strategies by female leaders can have the opposite effect of lowering female leaders' effectiveness. As is suggested also from the results of the experimental research previously described, when a leader's gender matches the task and leadership role, it may be more effective to behave explicitly and directly. On the other hand, however, given that extremely male-congenial behaviour (pressure P behaviour) has lower effectiveness than that of male leaders, when behaviour violates gender norms, this is thought to invite a negative outcome even if the circumstances are suited to female leaders.

Another field study is a survey conducted by the author in 2001 in male-dominant workplaces where the type of work was male-congenial, men accounted for an overwhelming majority of constituent members, and the ratio of women in the managerial echelon was extremely small. Even in such organisations, departments to which female managers (equivalent to sub-section chiefs) were assigned all had a comparatively large number of female employees, and were departments involved in gender-neutral or female-congenial types of work (general affairs, human resources, sales, and so on). When the author singled out from among departments with men in managerial positions those which were equivalent in terms of group size and type of work to departments with female managers, 190 employees (eight-six males, 104 females) representing a total of twenty-six departments—thirteen with female managers, and thirteen with male managers—ultimately became the target of analysis. These workers were made to assess their bosses' PM leadership behaviour as well as to evaluate various morale variables (employees' own motivation, departmental group meetings and the performance norms of the department).

First, as for leadership behaviour, when a two-way (bosses' gender × respondents' gender) MANOVA was performed, the main effect of bosses' gender on M behaviour was marginally significant, and the frequency of M behaviour tended to be higher in the case of female bosses than male bosses. In addition, when a three-way (bosses' gender × pressure P × M) MANOVA was conducted on various morale variables, the interaction of the three factors was significant vis-à-vis group meetings and performance norms. Regardless of the induced variables, female bosses with strong pressure P brought about a more advantageous effect when this was accompanied by M behaviour than when it was not, but in the case of male bosses with strong pressure P, such a tendency was not to be seen. Moreover, in cases of high pressure P and low M, male bosses were more effective than female bosses (see Figure 3.2). This result supports the hypothetical model, and suggests that in male-dominant workplaces, masculine behaviour (pressure P) which is not accompanied by female-congenial behaviour (in this case, M) diminishes female leaders' effectiveness. As for the prediction that women will find

Figure 3.2: The interaction effect of bosses' gender, pressure P and M behaviour on performance norm scores

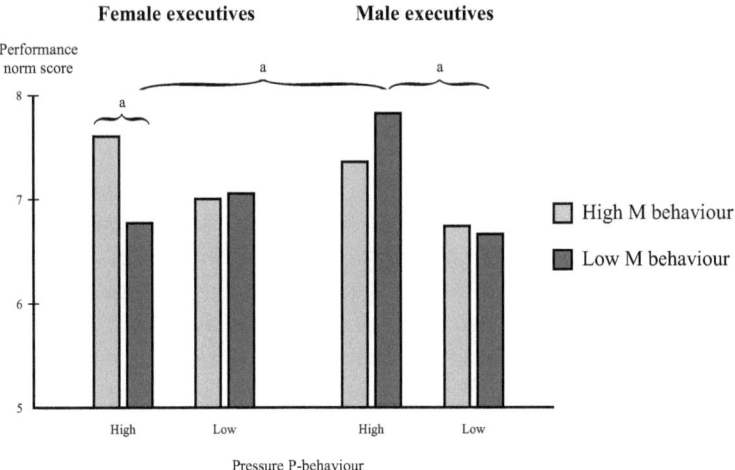

a: $p < .05$

it difficult to engage in feminine behaviour in male-dominant organisations, however, the result indicating that female leaders are more in the habit of engaging in M behaviour than are male leaders does not support it. This is thought to have been caused by the non-presence of particularly strong masculine behavioural norms, as the organisations which constituted the target of the study in question may have been male-dominant when seen from the perspective of organisations as a whole, but were comparatively female-dominant in terms of the types of work undertaken by the departments in which female managers were placed and the numerical ratio of males to females.

In summary, it can be argued that the results obtained from experimental studies do support—albeit only partially—my hypothesis as to the effect which the gender congeniality of tasks exerts upon leadership effectiveness. Results pertaining to administrative institutions have shown that female leaders' male-congenial behaviour (pressure P) has a negative effect on subordinate groups, regardless of whether it is accompanied by female-congenial behaviour (M), and that female leaders' use of indirect (female-congenial) strategies reduces subordinates' motivation. In terms of the hypothesis, this is a result which applies more to female leaders in male-dominant organisations.

Conversely, the result in corporate entities showed that if accompanied by M behaviour, female leaders' pressure P behaviour has a similarly positive effect on subordinate groups to that of male leaders. In the survey results of Takahashi et al. (1998), it was illustrated that corporate entities were more male-dominant than administrative institutions, but if it is understood that male-dominance was higher in administrative bodies than in the other types of organisations in the two field studies which this author conducted, it can be argued that the results obtained can be interpreted according to the hypothesis. As the degree of male dominance varies greatly between the organisations as a whole and the departments which have women in managerial positions, in future surveys it will probably be necessary to ascertain how female managers and their subordinates personally have perceived the situation in the workplace. As the number of female managers in male-dominant departments is extremely small, though, such a survey would be exceedingly difficult. On this point, we will need to wait for future surveys.

In Japan, one hardly sees any work which examines the effect of interaction between organisational or group factors and individual factors. If we may cite the breadth and flexibility of leaders' repertoire of leadership behaviour as an important individual factor, then the present situation in which the majority of women have little professional experience constitutes a serious problem, as can be seen from the results of the survey by the Japan Institute for Workers' Evolution mentioned at the beginning of this chapter. In Japan, having experience of various different departments and jobs within the one enterprise is often a condition for promotion to managerial rank, and such experience is regarded as enhancing the knowledge and skills necessary for managerial positions. Naturally, such personnel reshuffling often includes job transfers which involve moving house, and the reality is that in the current situation, in which women shoulder most of the responsibility for the home, married women's job transfers are often extremely difficult. For women, there may be a need for alternative systems for fostering breadth and flexibility in the leadership behaviour repertoire, apart from job-transfers which involve moving house.

Prospects for the future

In this chapter, I proposed a hypothetical model which could be conceived from the results of previous studies. There are, however, several points not as yet thoroughly explored which should be elucidated in future. The first is the issue of whether male dominance at the organisational level or male dominance at the departmental level where female leaders are assigned exerts a greater influence on gender differences in leadership effectiveness when the two types are in conflict, as seen in the results of the research on corporate entities discussed in the previous section. Prior studies have hardly touched upon this issue, but it is likely to become an important point when taking on-site measures to enhance the effectiveness of female leaders.

The second point involves the examination of dimensions of leadership other than task-orientation versus relationship-orientation. For example, though I did not discuss it in detail in this chapter, a gender difference has been found which is comparatively unaffected by situational influences, namely that female leaders are consistently stronger than male leaders in connection with transformational leadership behaviour (Eagly et al. 2003). There will probably be a future need to clarify such issues as whether such a gender disparity is really unaffected by factors on an organisational or group level, or whether this is really conducive to the enhancement of the effectiveness of female leaders. Moreover, the exploration of how gender differences in leadership effectiveness are predicted from the framework of LMX theory or social-constructivist leadership studies will also be a task for the future.

The third point is the elucidation of the possibility of female leaders' effectiveness to surpass that of males, and the mechanism involved in that instance. In most previous research, attention has mainly been focused upon the mechanism in which the effectiveness of female leaders lags behind that of male leaders, but there are actually several studies which demonstrate empirically that female leaders' effectiveness actually does outstrip that of male leaders. Even in the meta-analysis of Eagly et al. (1995), it is shown that female leaders have greater effectiveness than their male counterparts in business, educational and administrative organisations. From the viewpoint of social-role theory, Eagly et al. (1995) attribute the obtaining of a result such as this to the leadership role being comparatively congenial to women in these organisations. Might not the following mechanisms also be imaginable, however? In other words, in cases where organisational or group factors such as the male congeniality of tasks and leadership roles or men's numerical superiority; women's low status in society; and the presence of gender stereotypes are recognised by followers (or evaluators) as 'factors which impede the advancement of women to managerial positions,' it will potentially be recognised that 'women who have advanced in such adverse circumstances are superior in terms of ability to men of the same occupational rank' and the legitimacy of such women be perceived as being higher rather than lower than that of male leaders. The elucidation of the likelihood of the augmentation principle functioning in causal attribution for women's occupation of leadership roles and its regulating factors would also probably be useful for enhancing women's leadership effectiveness. Oddly enough, though this phenomenon is theoretically possible to predict, there has not been much research into the circumstances in which the phenomenon arises.

In this chapter, I have proposed a hypothetical model constituting a framework for use when considering the leadership effectiveness of female and male leaders. In Japan from now on, there will probably be a need especially to substantiate the interaction effect between organisational or group factors and individual factors.

4 Education, Employment and Gender Ideology

Kunihiro Kimura

Introduction: the aim of this chapter

The aim of this chapter is to explain the frequently-reported, apparently paradoxical relationships among the level of educational attainment, employment status and gender ideology of Japanese married women. None of the pre-existing theories concerning the associations among the three variables can explain these 'paradoxical' relationships, but I will venture to do so by proposing a new hypothesis of 'rational choice and cognitive dissonance under the constraint of the segmented labour market.' I will also show evidence from analysis of the relationship between high-school students' educational aspirations and their gender ideology.

Japanese wives' education, work and gender ideology

First of all, I point out that we frequently observe associations among Japanese married women's educational attainment, employment, and gender ideology,[1] as shown in Figure 4.1. Gender ideology is usually measured by a survey question which asks married women whether they agree or disagree with the statement: 'Men should work outside (the home), and (married) women should stay home.' There is a negative association between educational attainment and attitudes towards the gendered division of labour, a negative association between these attitudes and employment, and also a negative association between educational attainment and employment.

Some readers might be surprised at the negative association between education and employment, because this differs from the situation in Western societies (and also in Taiwan) (Brinton 1993, 2001; Brinton, Lee and Parish 1995; Choe, Bumpass and Tsuya 2004;

Figure 4.1: Associations among educational attainment, employment, and gender ideology for Japanese married women

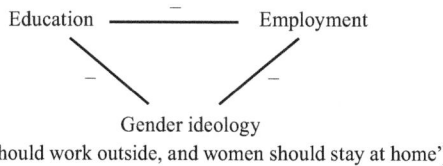

Gender ideology
('Men should work outside, and women should stay at home')

Molm 1978; Smith-Lovin and Tickamyer 1978). Rather than focusing on that association, however, I prefer to explain the apparently paradoxical associations among these three variables as a whole.[2]

Data: HIGH5/SSM95 Surveys

For this purpose, I use mainly the following two datasets: one comprises data from the fifth survey on 'Social Consciousness of High-School Students and Their Parents,' conducted by the Work Group on Education and Culture, Tohoku University. In the following discussion, I call this survey by its nickname, 'HIGH5 Survey.' The data were collected in November and December 2003 by means of self-administered questionnaires. The planned samples were 1,280 second-year students from ten high schools in Sendai, Japan, and their parents. The proportions of returned questionnaires were eighty-seven per cent for students, fifty-six per cent for 'fathers,' and sixty-nine per cent for 'mothers.'

The other dataset comprised data from the fifth survey on 'Social Stratification and Social Mobility' in Japan. Its nickname, SSM95, is well-known in Japan. The data were collected in October and November 1995. Three types of questionnaires, that is, A, B, and Prestige, were used in this survey. The planned samples were 9,730 Japanese adults aged twenty to sixty-nine years. I use the data from married female respondents aged thirty to fifty-nine in Questionnaires A and B—Questionnaire A having been designed mainly to measure social mobility, that is, inter- and intra-generational mobility, while Questionnaire B aimed to explore the relationship between the structure of social stratification and people's social attitudes. Fortunately, however, the items which I will use in this chapter were contained in both of the questionnaires. The effective sample size was 1,716.

Results for married women

In the data from the HIGH5 Survey, we can observe the paradoxical associations mentioned above among education, employment and gender ideology for 'mothers' aged thirty-six to fifty-five. Figure 4.2 shows the association between their educational attainment and their employment status. The percentage of homemakers who have attained a higher education is greater than that of those who have not.[3] Figure 4.3 shows the negative associations between education and gender ideology, and between employment status and gender ideology for 'mothers' aged thirty-six to fifty-five. The proportion of those who approve of the gendered division of labour tends to be smaller among married women who have gained a higher education than among those who have not, regardless of their employment status. Homemakers tend to be the first to approve of the gendered division of labour, while full-time workers are likely to be the last to approve of it, regardless of their educational attainment.

We can also observe the paradoxical associations among education, employment and gender ideology for married women aged thirty to fifty-nine by using the data from the SSM95 Survey. Figure 4.4 shows the association between their educational attainment and employment status. The percentage of homemakers who have gained a higher education is greater than that of ones who have not, especially in the case of married women aged forty to forty-nine. Figure 4.5 shows the negative associations between education and gender ideology, and between employment status and gender ideology for married women aged thirty to fifty-nine, respectively.

We thus can confirm the paradoxical associations among the three variables for married women, by using our HIGH5 and SSM95 Survey datasets. See Appendix 4A for the results of more sophisticated analysis of our data using hierarchical log-linear modelling.

Pre-existing theories

I will show that none of the pre-existing theories concerning these associations can explain their 'paradoxical' nature. We can cite at least four such theories or theses, as follows:[4]
  1. Enlightenment and rationalisation (social psychological studies) (e.g. Hara and Hiwano 1990)
  2. Human capital or signalling (educational economics) (Becker 1993 (1964); Spence 1974)

Figure 4.2: Employment status of married women ('mothers' aged 36–55) by educational attainment [HIGH5]

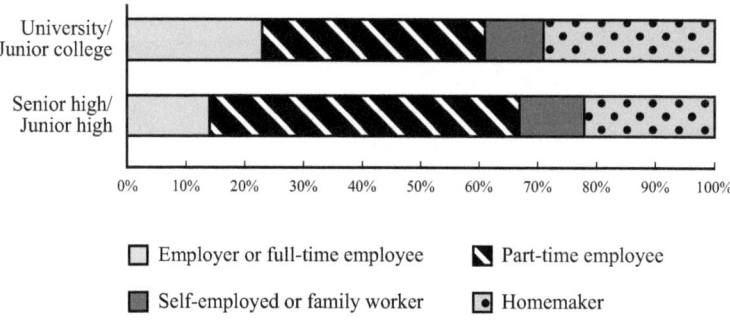

Note: Home-workers (*naishokusha*) are regarded as a kind of part-time employee because they are in the marginal labour market.

Figure 4.3: Percentages of married women ('mothers' aged 36–55) agreeing that 'men should work outside, and women should stay home,' by education and employment status [HIGH5]

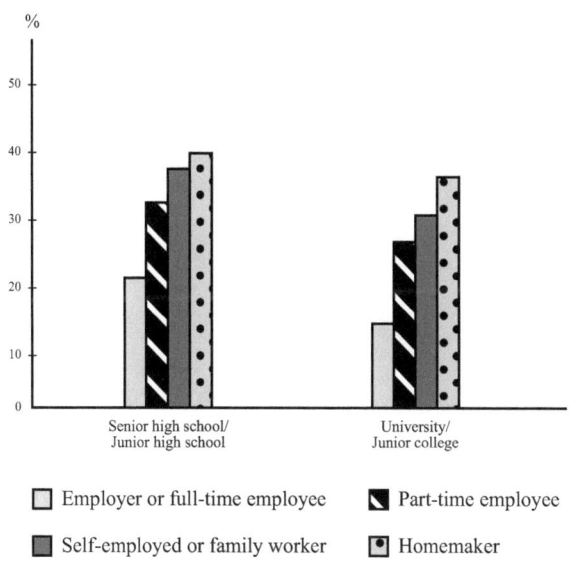

Note: Home-workers (*naishokusha*) are regarded as a kind of part-time employee because they are in the marginal labour market.

Figure 4.4: Employment status of married women by age-group and education [SSM95]

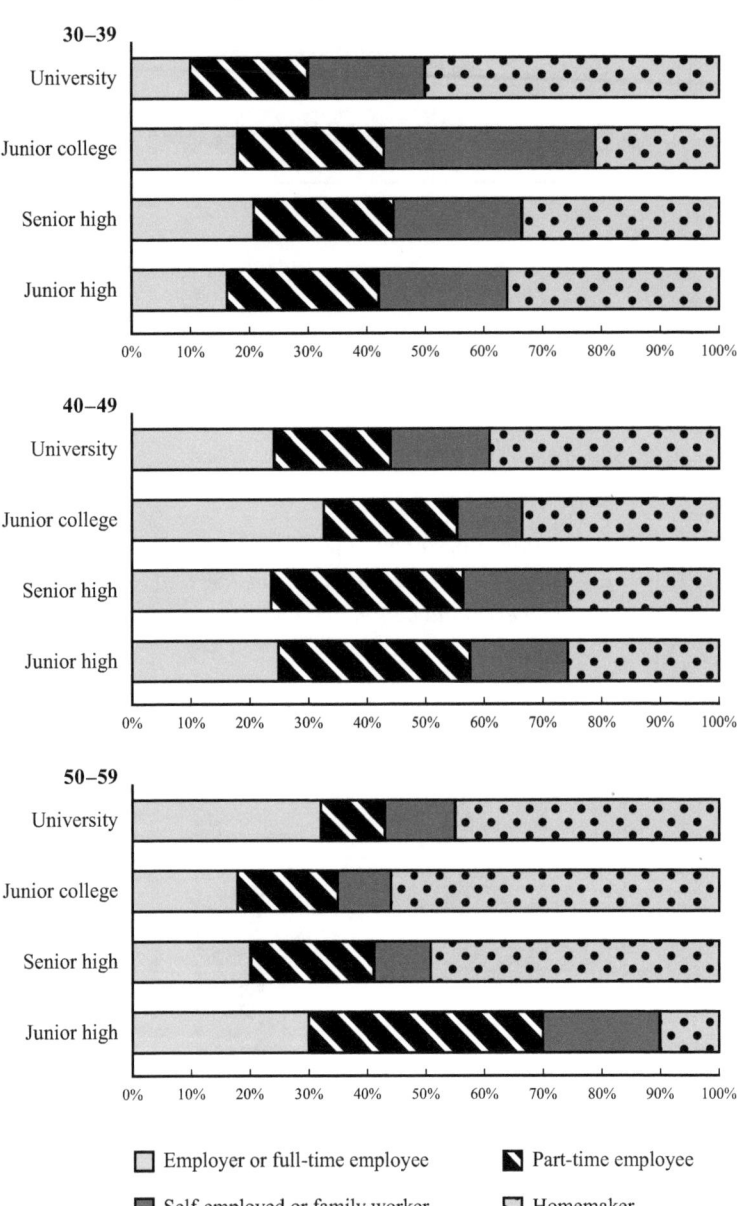

Note: Home-workers (*naishokusha*) are regarded as a kind of part-time employee because they are in the marginal labour market.

Education, Employment and Gender Ideology 89

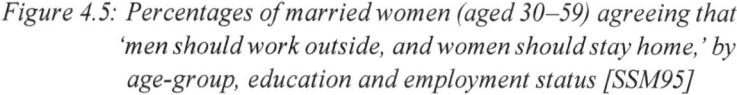

Figure 4.5: Percentages of married women (aged 30–59) agreeing that 'men should work outside, and women should stay home,' by age-group, education and employment status [SSM95]

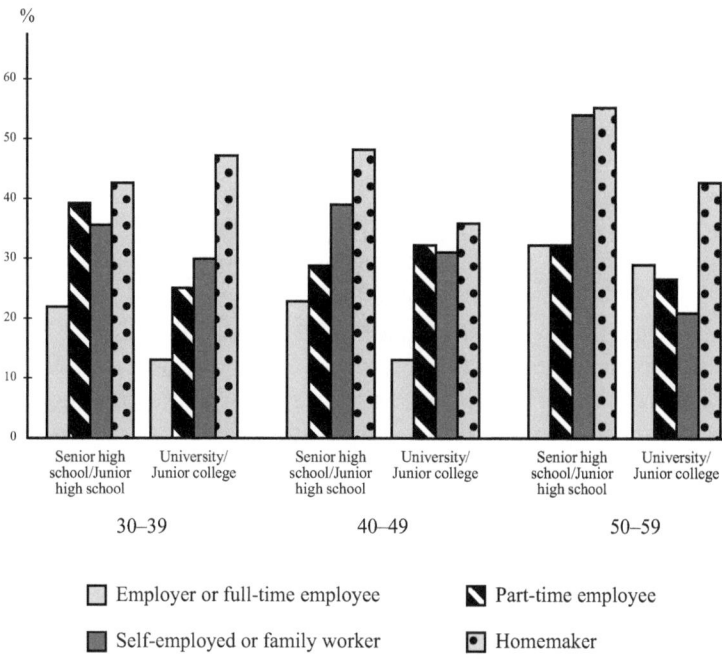

Note: Home-workers (*naishokusha*) are regarded as a kind of part-time employee because they are in the marginal labour market.

3. Advantage in the marriage market (e.g. Wakisaka 1990; cf. Douglas 1964 (1934, 1957))
4. Gender difference in the meaning of higher education and the reproduction of gender stereotypes by socialisation ('general education' for women) (e.g. Brinton 1993)

Let us see how these theories fail to explain the associations among the three variables as a whole.

Enlightenment and rationalisation

First, let us focus on the thesis of enlightenment and rationalisation. The essence of this thesis is expressed as the diagram in Panel a of Figure 4.6. This thesis is a variant of sociological and social psychological theories which regard both education and employment as determinants of gender ideology (e.g. Molm 1978; Thornton, Alwin and Camburn 1983; Thornton and Freedman 1979; cf. Tallichet and Willis 1986). Hara and Hiwano (1990), for example, argue that higher education promotes not only critical attitudes towards the *status quo* of the society in general, but also critical attitudes towards the gendered division of labour. On the other hand, they assume that people have a tendency to rationalise their own employment status. This thesis cannot, however, tell how education and employment are associated with each other.

Human capital or signalling
The second thesis I examine is derived from educational economics, that is, 'human capital theory' or 'signalling theory.' From the point of view of educational economics, higher education is a spring-board for occupational attainment and life-long work/career. Thus, if we assume that female high-school students' gender ideology reflects their preferences, then entering university would be rational for those who disapproved of the gendered division of labour and whose families could afford the costs. The causal relations predicted by this thesis are expressed as the diagram in Panel b of Figure 4.6. This thesis cannot explain the negative association between education and employment for Japanese married women, however.

Advantage in the marriage market
Some other economists thus emphasise the significance or advantage of higher education for women in the marriage market. The diagram in Panel c of Figure 4.6 shows the causal relations predicted by this 'marriage market thesis' (e.g. Wakisaka 1990). Wakisaka's argument (1990) is in part inspired by Douglas's (1964 (1934, 1957)) classical work.

The marriage market thesis argues as follows: women who support the gendered division of labour will tend to enter universities (or junior colleges—which typically offer two-year undergraduate courses, in contrast to the four or more years of study at most universities), and such female university (or junior-college) graduates tend to marry male university graduates whose incomes are high. This would be the advantage of higher education for women, especially in Japan.[5] Consequently, most female university (or junior-college) graduates need not work in order to maintain their higher living standards.[6]

Yet the marriage market thesis fails to explain the negative association between gender ideology and educational attainment. As we will see, there is little evidence indicating that Japanese women try to attain higher education specifically because entering a university

Figure 4.6: Causal diagrams predicted by pre-existing theories

a. Enlightenment and rationalism

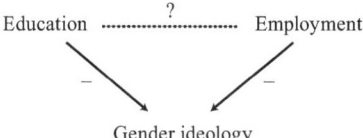

b. Human capital or signalling

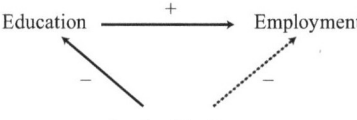

c. Advantage in the marriage market

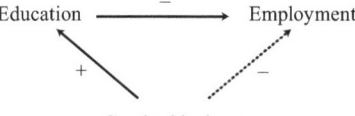

d. 'General education' for women

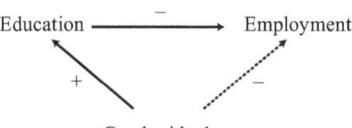

Note: a broken arrow-line indicates that there may or may not be a causal relation between the two variables.

(or a junior college) would enhance their chances of marrying a male university graduate with a high income.

'General education' for women

Let us move on to the fourth thesis, which emphasises the difference between men and women in the meaning of higher education (e.g. Brinton 1993). Brinton (1993: 204–217) says that, in Japan, '[p]arents are likely to view university education as job-preparation for sons and general education for daughters.' Parents socialise their sons and daughters differently, through educational aspiration and investment, because parents recognise that there exists severe sex discrimination in the labour market in Japan. As a consequence of such socialisation, those sons and daughters become 'typical' male and female young adults—that is, they accept the gendered division of labour. Employers thus expect that women will quit their jobs at marriage or upon childbirth, and so they prefer men to women when hiring employees and 'assign women to jobs that involve little on-the-job training and few career prospects.' Such employers' practices feed back to the socialisation of the next generation (Brinton 1993: 96–99).

The diagram in Panel d of Figure 4.6 shows the causal relations among the education, employment and gender ideology of Japanese married women as predicted by this thesis. This thesis cannot, however, explain the negative association which exists between gender ideology and educational attainment among Japanese married women.

How pre-existing theories fail: a summary

Table 4.1 summarises the predictions from the hypotheses above and the observed results. The thesis of enlightenment and rationalisation cannot tell how education and employment are associated with each other; neither can standard educational economics explain the negative association between education and employment for Japanese married women; and the marriage market thesis fails to explain the negative association between gender ideology and educational attainment. There is little evidence to indicate that Japanese women have tried to attain higher education specifically because entering a university (or a junior college) would enhance their chances of marrying a male university graduate, whose income would be high. The fourth thesis, which emphasises the difference in the meaning of higher education between men and women, cannot explain the negative association between gender ideology and educational attainment of Japanese married women.

Table 4.1: *Summary of predictions from pre-existing theories on the associations among the relevant variables*

	Married women (or 'mothers')		
	Edu–GI	Emp–GI	Edu–Emp
Enlightenment and rationalisation	–	–	?
Human capital or signalling	–	–	+
'Marriage market'	+	–	–
'General education'	+	–	–
Observation	–	–	–

Note: Edu = education; GI = gender ideology; Emp = employment

A new hypothesis: rational choice and cognitive dissonance

We have seen that none of the existing theories can explain the seemingly paradoxical associations among Japanese women's education, employment and gender ideology. I thus propose a new hypothesis which may explain these associations. It postulates rational choice and cognitive dissonance under the constraints of the segmented labour market.[7] It consists, moreover, of three parts which correspond to the various life-stages of Japanese women.

Stage 1: From high-school to university or work
In the first stage, that is, when women are lower- or upper-secondary-school students, they regard higher education as a spring-board for occupational attainment and life-long work/career. From this point of view, for some female students whose families can afford the costs, it is rational to enter a university. At this stage, it is those girls who are critical of the gendered division of labour rather than those who accept it who have a higher level of educational aspiration. For female high-school students who are critical of the gendered division of labour, then, the premise of educational economics seems to hold.

Stage 2: In the segmented labour market
In the second stage, however—that is, after graduating from high schools or universities—women suffer from the constraints of the segmented labour market in Japan (cf. Horne-Kawashima 1985; Kawashima and Tachibanaki 1986). As a result, most women face a gap between their aspirations and reality, and so they experience

cognitive dissonance (cf. Festinger 1957; Harmon-Jones and Mills 1999; Thibodeau and Aronson 1992). On the one hand, highly-educated women tend to enter the full-time sector, but there exist both 'statistical discrimination' (Phelps 1972) and a 'marriage bar.'[8] Employers (especially large firms) expect that women will tend to quit their jobs at marriage or upon childbirth, and employers consequently prefer male university graduates to female university- or junior-college graduates when hiring full-time workers. Moreover, even if female university- or junior-college graduates succeed in being hired as full-time workers, the environment of workplaces is not favourable to married women, and so the latter will have to quit their job at marriage or upon childbirth. On the other hand, at such junctures, women who lack a higher education tend to enter the part-time sector, where both quitting a job and re-entering the sector are easy. Most women thus face a gap between their aspirations and reality,[9] which results in cognitive dissonance.[10]

Stage 3: After marriage/birth resignation or labour market re-entry
In the third stage, women who experience cognitive dissonance try to reduce it by rationalising their employment status and changing their gender ideology in a way that is compatible with their employment status (cf. Mason, Czajka and Arber 1976: 575; Molm 1978: 523). This is because the experience of cognitive dissonance is so uncomfortable that it generates psychological pressure to reduce it.[11]

I predict that, as a result, the magnitude of the negative association between married women's education and gender ideology will become smaller than that of the negative association between female high-school students' educational aspiration and gender ideology—notice, however, that I postulate here that the negative association between such students' educational aspiration and gender ideology is *so strong* that the association between married women's education and gender ideology would not become positive even after the reduction of cognitive dissonance. If we had assumed that the association between married women's education and gender ideology could be positive, the falsifiability of this new hypothesis would be spoiled.

In summary, this hypothesis of rational choice and cognitive dissonance under the constraint of a segmented labour market predicts the following causal relationship among educational attainment, employment and gender ideology for Japanese married women, as in the diagram in Figure 4.7.

Figure 4.7: A causal diagram predicted by the hypothesis of rational choice and cognitive dissonance under the constraint of a segmented labour market

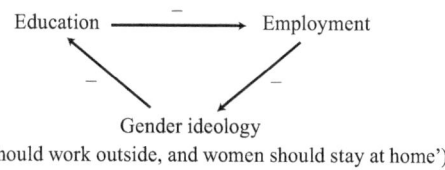

Gender ideology
('Men should work outside, and women should stay at home')

Evidence from analysis of female high-school students' attitudes

I will now present evidence which supports my hypothesis by analysing female high-school students' attitudes. There is a negative association between gender ideology and educational aspiration, and also between gender ideology and aspiration towards work/career, but there is a positive association between educational aspiration and work/career aspiration.

Figure 4.8 shows the negative association between gender ideology and educational aspiration. The percentage of female students who would like to enter a university, for example, is greater among those who disapprove of the gendered division of labour than among those who accept it.

Figure 4.9 shows the negative association between gender ideology and aspiration for work/career. Forty-two per cent of those who disapprove of the gendered division of labour would like to continue to work after marriage or childbirth, while only twelve per cent of those who approve of it would like to do so.

Figure 4.10 shows the positive association between educational- and work/career aspirations after controlling for gender ideology. The percentage of those desiring to enter a university among those female high-school students who would like to work after marriage or childbirth (to continue to work; or to quit their job initially, but later return to work) is greater than the percentage of those wishing to enter a university among those female high-school students who would like to quit their jobs at marriage or childbirth, regardless of their gender ideology.

I also conducted additional analyses using the datasets of high-school students and their 'mothers' or married women collected in the 1990s and 1980s: analyses of the datasets of the fourth and third surveys on 'Social Consciousness of High-School Students

Figure 4.8: Female high-school students' attitude towards the gendered division of labour and their educational aspirations [HIGH5]

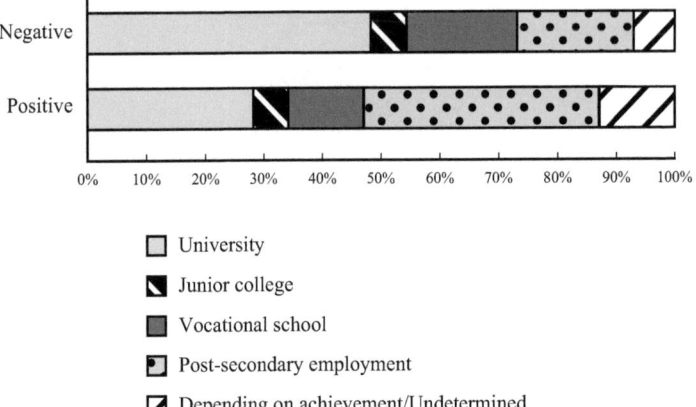

☐ University
◨ Junior college
■ Vocational school
⦿ Post-secondary employment
▨ Depending on achievement/Undetermined

Note: A vocational school (*senmon-gakkō*) is a post-secondary school which provides students with specialised and practical courses for vocational education.

Figure 4.9: Female high-school students' attitude towards the gendered division of labour and their work/career aspirations [HIGH5]

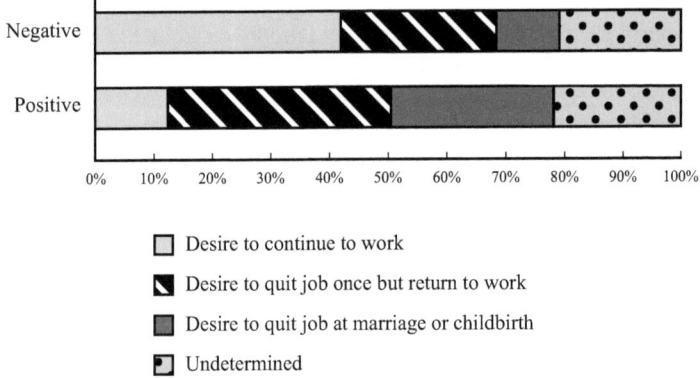

☐ Desire to continue to work
◨ Desire to quit job once but return to work
■ Desire to quit job at marriage or childbirth
⦿ Undetermined

and Their Parents' (1999 and 1994); a secondary analysis of the data from a survey of senior high-school students (in their twelfth year of schooling) in Hyogo Prefecture in 1981 and 1982; and an analysis of

Figure 4.10: Percentages of female high-school students desiring to enter university, by work/career aspiration and attitude towards the gendered division of labour [HIGH5]

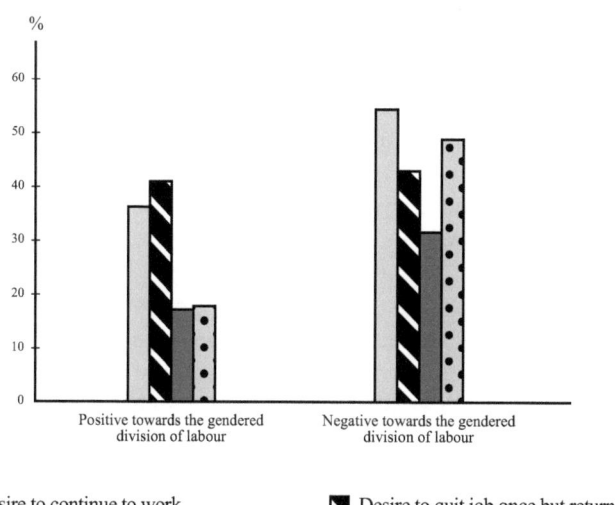

☐ Desire to continue to work ◨ Desire to quit job once but return to work
▤ Desire to quit job at marriage or childbirth ⦿ Undetermined

the SSM85 survey. (These kinds of analysis could be called 'Back to the Future'-type strategies.) I found that similar results were obtained for these datasets (Kimura 1998; Kimura 2005). Figures 4.11 and 4.12, for example, show the results of secondary analysis of the data from a survey of high-school students in Hyogo Prefecture in 1981 and 1982. (The cohort of the high-school students roughly corresponds to the respondents aged thirty-one or thirty-two in the SSM95 Survey and to those aged thirty-nine or forty in the HIGH5 Survey—though, strictly speaking, the populations of these three surveys are different from each other.) Because the questionnaire in the survey does not contain any item to measure gender ideology directly, I analysed the associations between high-school students' educational aspirations, on the one hand, and their evaluations of the importance of their prospects for future jobs and the importance of their concern for marriage, on the other.

We can observe a positive association between female high-school students' educational aspirations and their perceived importance of prospects for a future job. The percentage of those who would like to enter universities was thirty-six per cent among female high-school students who thought that prospects for their future job were important in deciding their own course after graduating from high school, while the percentage of would-be university entrants was twenty-seven per cent among girls at high school who saw prospects for their future job as not important. The percentage of those wishing to work after secondary-school graduation was twenty-one per cent among female high-school students who gave importance to prospects for their future job, while the percentage of those desiring to work after graduating from high school was forty-five per cent among female high-school students who regarded future job prospects as unimportant.

Moreover, we can observe a relatively negative association between female high-school students' educational aspirations and their concern vis-à-vis marriage. The proportion of those who would like to enter universities was twenty-eight per cent among female high-school students who thought that their concern towards marriage was important in deciding their own life-course after graduating from high school, while the proportion of those wanting to enter universities accounted for thirty-nine per cent of female high-school students for whom concern for marriage was not important. The proportion of those who desired to work after high-school graduation was twenty-eight per cent among female high-school students who considered their concern vis-à-vis marriage to be important, while the proportion of those wishing to work after graduating from high school was twenty-three per cent of high-school girls who thought that their concern for marriage was unimportant.

It is worth noting that the degree of association between female high-school students' evaluation of prospects for their future job and that of their concern towards marriage in deciding their own life-course after graduating from secondary school was almost zero ($r = 0.055$). These results suggest to us that the relationship between educational aspiration and gender ideology for female high-school students in the early 1980s and that for their present-day counterparts are similar.

Table 4.2 summarises the predictions from the hypotheses I have examined and the observed results. I emphasise that the observed results equate only with the predictions from my hypothesis, which postulates rational choice and cognitive dissonance under the constraint of the segmented labour market.

Figure 4.11: Female high-school students' responses to the question whether job prospects are important in deciding their own post-secondary life-course and their educational aspirations [Hyogo Prefecture, 1981–1982]

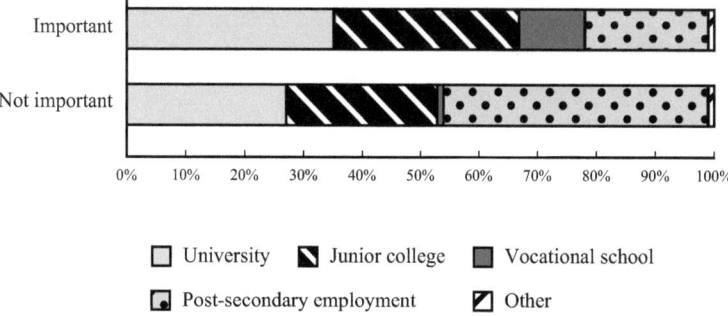

Note: A vocational school (*senmon-gakkō*) is a post-secondary school which provides students with specialised and practical courses for vocational education.

Figure 4.12: Female high-school students' responses to the question whether marriage is important in deciding their own post-secondary life-course and their educational aspirations [Hyogo Prefecture, 1981–1982]

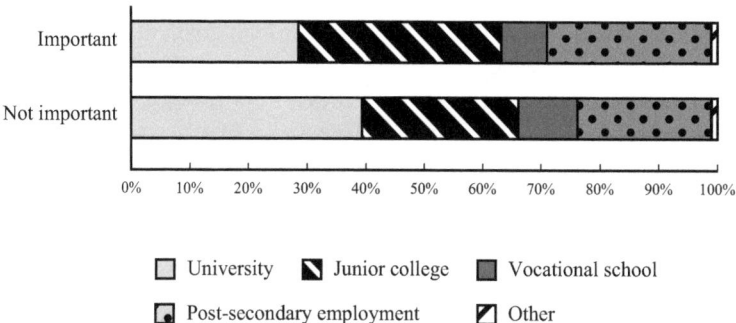

Note: A vocational school (*senmon-gakkō*) is a post-secondary school which provides students with specialised and practical courses for vocational education.

Table 4.2: Summary of predictions on associations among relevant variables from theories and observed associations

	Married women ('mothers')			Female students
	Edu–GI	Emp–GI	Edu–Emp	GI–EA
Enlightenment and rationalisation	–	–	?	0?
Human capital or signalling	–	–	+	–
'Marriage market'	+	–	–	+
'General education'	+	–	–	+
Rational choice and cognitive dissonance in the segmented labour market	– (Weak)	–	–	– (Strong)
Observation	–	–	–	–

Note: Edu = education; GI = gender ideology; Emp = employment; EA = educational aspirations

Discussion

I realise that my argument has some issues to resolve. One of the most serious of these is that the negative association between gender ideology and education may be spurious. In fact, after the introduction either of the various types or levels of high schools or tracks (general schools or tracks with a high rate of advancement to universities or junior colleges/general schools or tracks with a moderate advancement rate to universities or junior colleges/vocational training schools or tracks with a low rate of advancement to universities or junior colleges), or of parents' educational attainment as the 'third variable,' the association between gender ideology and educational aspiration almost disappears. For example, as Figure 4.13 shows, *if the types or levels of high schools or tracks are the same*, then the percentages of female high-school students desiring to enter a university are almost the same regardless of their attitude towards the gendered division of labour, though the percentage of female high-school students desiring to enter a university varies with the types or levels of high school or tracks.

Moreover, we can observe positive associations between parents' educational attainment and the types or levels of high schools which female students attend. For example, the proportion of female students in general schools or tracks with a high rate of advancement to universities or junior colleges is forty-three per cent among girls

Figure 4.13: Percentages of female high-school students desiring to enter a university, by gender ideology and types or levels of high schools or tracks [HIGH5]

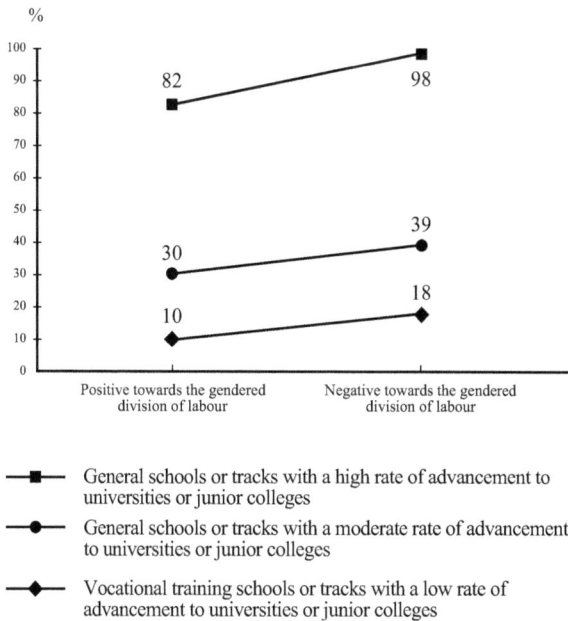

whose fathers attained a higher education, while the proportion of female students in general schools or tracks with a high rate of advancement to universities or junior colleges is fourteen per cent among girls whose fathers have not attained a higher education. This indicates that fathers' educational attainment has a direct effect on the types or levels of high schools their children attend, and, in turn, the types or levels of high schools have a direct, positive effect on female high-school students' educational aspirations and a direct negative effect on their gender ideology, at the same time.[12]

Therefore, the revised version of the hypothetical causal diagram in Figure 4.14 is a plausible one, and this suggests that there may be little room for rational choice and cognitive dissonance reduction. This is a serious problem for my argument.

Another difficulty is that my hypothesis of rational choice and cognitive dissonance under the constraint of the segmented labour market cannot explain the well-known fact that there have been differences between female and male university (or junior-college)

Figure 4.14: A hypothetical causal diagram for relevant variables in the typical life-course for Japanese married women

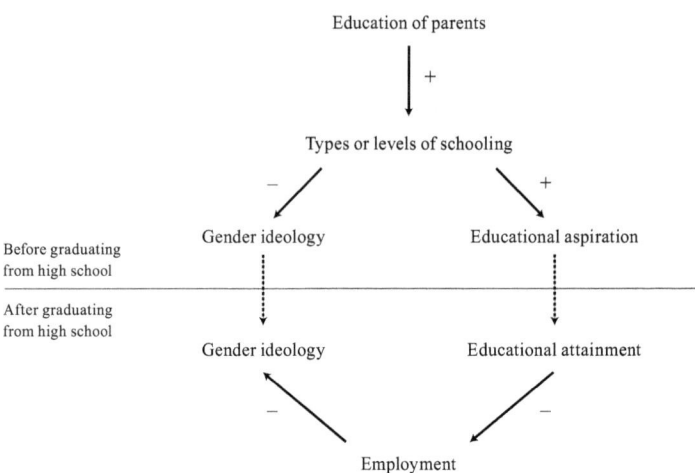

Note: A normal arrow indicates that the causal relation between the two variables is inferred by the analyses in this chapter. A broken arrow-line indicates that the causal relation between the two variables could be examined only by analysis of data from a panel survey.

students, not only in the proportion of those who gain a higher education, but also in the majors or disciplines studied (although the disparity in the former case has decreased). Of course, the marriage market thesis or Brinton's (1993) argument which emphasises the difference in the meaning of higher education for women and men might explain the difference in the chosen majors or disciplines between male and female university (or junior-college) students. We can, however, observe these gender differences not only in Japan, but also in other industrial countries and areas, including the United States, and we know that sociologists and educational economists have tried to explain why such gender differences persist (e.g. Arai 1998 (1995): 141–147; Hara and Seiyama 2005 (1999): 122–129; Polachek 1978). Moreover, as we have seen, both the marriage market thesis and Brinton's (1993) argument fail to explain the paradoxical associations between Japanese married women's education, employment and gender ideology. Therefore, I do not think that the marriage market thesis or Brinton's (1993) argument is superior to the hypothesis of rational choice and cognitive dissonance under the constraint of the segmented labour market.

In addition, because the hypothesis of rational choice and cognitive dissonance under the constraint of the segmented labour market focuses on the relationship among education, employment and gender ideology which appears regardless of cohort or historical period, this hypothesis disregards the period- and cohort effects on the education, employment and gender ideology of Japanese women, which we can confirm by comparing the results of SSM85, SSM95 and other surveys (cf. Ojima 2000). We should pay more attention to the historical background of Japanese women's situation in order to improve our theoretical arguments and data analyses.

Conclusion

In this chapter, I first described the apparently paradoxical relationship among educational attainment, employment status, and gender ideology among Japanese married women. In order to explain these 'paradoxical' associations, I proposed a hypothesis of 'rational choice and cognitive dissonance under the constraint of the segmented labour market.' I also showed evidence to support my hypothesis through analysis of the relationship between high-school students' educational aspirations and their gender ideology, using a 'Back to the Future'-type research strategy. My hypothesis seems superior to pre-existing theories in its explanatory power, in a theoretical sense.

I do admit, however, that my hypothesis has some difficulties. The negative association between gender ideology and education may be spurious. My hypothesis cannot explain the well-known fact that there have been differences not only in the proportions of men and women who attain higher education, but also in the academic disciplines or majors pursued by female and male university (or junior-college) students. Moreover, my hypothesis disregards period- and cohort effects. Not only do we need further data analysis of panel surveys if the datasets are available, or of other kinds of surveys that enable us to conduct (quasi-)cohort analysis, but also elaboration of theoretical argument in order to envisage a more valid hypothesis.

Acknowledgments

The datasets of the fourth and fifth surveys on 'Social Stratification and Social Mobility' in Japan are used by permission of the Association for the Social Stratification and Social Mobility Survey 1995. The datasets of the third through fifth surveys of 'Social Consciousness of High-School Students and Their Parents' are used by permission of the Work Group on Education and Culture, Tohoku University. I thank Fumiaki Ojima for permitting me to use the dataset of a survey of high-school students in Hyogo Prefecture in 1981 and 1982. Earlier versions of this paper were presented at the Second International Conference on Rational Choice and Social Institutions, March 9–11, 2005, at the University of Groningen, Groningen, The Netherlands, and the Third US-Japan Joint Conference on Mathematical Sociology, June 24–26, 2005, at Hokkaido University in Sapporo, Japan.

Appendix 4A: Results of hierarchical log-linear analyses

Let us examine whether the associations among the educational attainment, employment status and gender ideology of Japanese married women are statistically significant, by means of hierarchical log-linear analysis of the data from SSM95 and HIGH5 Surveys.

The stepwise procedure for the hierarchical log-linear analysis is as follows (e.g. Agresti [1990] 2002: chaps. 8–9; Agresti 1996: chap. 6; Wickens 1989): we start with the saturated model, which includes the term for the highest order of interaction. In the following steps, we compare the present model with simpler models which eliminate one of the highest-order interaction terms contained in the present model. In this comparison, we calculate the difference in the likelihood ratio chi-square statistics (ΔG^2) between the present model and a simpler model. If we have some simpler models such that the P-values for the ΔG^2s are greater than 0.05, that is, if adopting the simpler models instead of the present model will not cause a statistically-significant change in the fit for the data, then we will select the simpler model with the greatest P-value, and go on to the next step. If all of the P-values for the ΔG^2s between the present model and the simpler models which eliminate one of the highest-order interaction terms contained in the present model are smaller than 0.05, that is, if replacing a simpler model for the present model will cause a statistically-significant change in the fit for the data, we will stop eliminating the highest-order interaction term(s), and select the present model as the most 'satisfactory' model.

Table 4A.1 shows the result of goodness-of-fit tests for hierarchical log-linear models relating to the education (E), employment or work status (W), and gender ideology or gender-role attitude (R) of 'mothers' (aged thirty-six to fifty-five) in HIGH5 datasets. The most 'satisfactory' model selected in the stepwise procedure is (EW, WR), that is, the model which contains both the term representing the

Table 4A.1: Goodness-of-fit tests for hierarchical log-linear models relating the education (E), employment or work status (W), and gender ideology or gender-role attitude (R) of 'mothers' (aged 36–55) [HIGH5]

Model	G^2	df	P-value	ΔG^2	df	P-value
(EWR)	–	–	–	–	–	–
(EW, ER, WR)#	0.328	3	0.955	0.328	3	0.955
(ER, WR)	20.433	6	0.002	20.105	3	0.000
(EW, ER)	20.166	6	0.003	19.838	3	0.000
(EW, WR)*	3.240	4	0.518	2.912	1	0.088

Note: E=education; W=employment or work status; R=gender ideology or gender-role attitude. The sign # shows that the model corresponds to frequently-reported results. The sign * shows the most 'satisfactory' model selected in the stepwise procedure ($N = 804$).

association between education and employment, and that representing the association between employment and gender ideology. However, if we have recourse to the AIC (Akaike Information Criterion) (Sakamoto, Ishiguro and Kitagawa 1986 (1983)), we will find that the model (EW, ER, WR), that is, the model which contains the terms for all the two-factor associations among education, employment and gender ideology, is more appropriate than the model (EW, WR). The value of the AIC for the model (EW, ER, WR) is −5.672, while that for the model (EW, WR) is −4.760, a lower AIC value indicating that the model is more appropriate.

Table 4A.2 shows the result of goodness-of-fit tests for hierarchical log-linear models relating to the education (E), employment or work status (W), gender ideology or gender-role attitude (R), and age (A) of married women aged thirty to fifty-nine in SSM95 datasets. The most 'satisfactory' model selected in the stepwise procedure is (EW, ER, WR, RA, WA, EA), that is, the model which contains the terms for all of the two-factor associations among education, employment, gender ideology and age, this result being replicated by examination using the AIC. It is thus safe to say that all of the two-factor associations among the educational attainment, employment status and gender ideology of Japanese married women do exist.

Let us turn to the associations among educational aspiration, aspiration towards work/career and gender ideology among female high-school students. Table 4A.3 shows the result of goodness-of-fit

Table 4A.2: *Goodness-of-fit tests for hierarchical log-linear models relating the education (E), employment or work status (W), gender ideology or gender-role attitude (R), and age (A) of married women (aged 30–59) [SSM95]*

Model	G^2	df	P-value	ΔG^2	df	P-value
(EWRA)	–	–	–	–	–	–
(EWR, EWA, ERA, WRA)	5.710	6	0.456	5.710	6	0.456
(EWR, ERA, EWA)	9.989	12	0.619	4.259	6	0.642
(EWR, EWA, RA)	11.193	14	0.671	1.224	2	0.542
(EWR, RA, WA, EA)	17.050	20	0.650	5.857	6	0.439
(EW, ER, WR, RA, WA, EA)#*	20.636	23	0.603	3.586	3	0.310

Note: E = education; W = employment or work status; R = gender ideology or gender-role attitude; A = age. The sign # shows that the model corresponds to frequently-reported results. The sign * shows the most 'satisfactory' model selected in the stepwise procedure (N = 1,696).

Table 4A.3: *Goodness-of-fit tests for hierarchical log-linear models relating the educational aspiration (E), aspiration for work/career (W), and gender ideology or gender-role attitude (R) of female high-school students [HIGH5]*

Model	G^2	df	P-value	ΔG^2	df	P-value
(EWR)	–	–	–	–	–	–
(EW, ER, WR)#	4.491	6	0.610	4.491	6	0.610
(EW, ER)	32.009	8	0.000	27.518	2	0.000
(ER, WR)	20.349	12	0.061	15.858	6	0.015
(EW, WR)*	9.807	9	0.366	5.315	3	0.150

Note: E = educational aspiration (excluding 'undetermined'); W = aspiration for work/career (excluding 'undetermined'); R = gender ideology or gender-role attitude. The sign # shows the model that would support my hypothesis. The sign * shows the most 'satisfactory' model selected in the stepwise procedure (N = 313).

tests for hierarchical log-linear models relating to the educational aspiration (E), aspiration for work/career (W) and gender ideology or gender-role attitude (R) of female high-school students in HIGH5 datasets. My hypothesis of 'rational choice and cognitive dissonance under the constraint of the segmented labour market' predicts that the model which contains the terms for all the two-factor associations among these three variables, that is, the model (EW, ER, WR), would be selected. The result, however, indicates that the most 'satisfactory' model to be selected in the stepwise procedure is (EW, WR), that is, the model which only contains the term representing the association between educational aspiration and aspiration for work/career, and that representing the association between work/career aspiration and gender ideology. Nevertheless, I do not think that the fit of the model (EW, ER, WR) for the data is especially bad, because the P-value for the ΔG^2 between that model and the saturated model is quite large, and the difference in the values of the AIC between the model (EW, ER, WR) and the model (EW, WR) is very small, the AIC value for the model (EW, WR) being −8.193, while that for the model (EW, ER, WR) is −7.509.

Appendix 4B: Rewards of education through marriage

In this appendix, I will calculate rough estimates of the economic returns of education though marriage for Japanese women, using the association between the husband's and wife's educational levels, on the one hand, and the mean income of the husband (tax included), on the other hand. In the following discussion, for simplicity, neither the financial cost of education nor the cost of marriage is considered.

Table 4B.1 shows the association between a husband's and a wife's educational levels in Japan. We can observe a strong tendency of homogamy with respect to education. I regard the column percentages in Panel b as the probabilities that a woman of a particular educational level will marry a man of each educational level.

Figure 4B.1 shows the mean income of the husband for all combinations of the wife's and husband's educational levels. Roughly speaking, the mean of the husband's income increases as both the husband's and wife's years of education increase. Notice, however, that the mean is not only sensitive to the values of the outliers but is also misleading as a measure of the central tendency where the distribution is skewed, as in the income distribution, and the median is therefore usually preferred to the mean for descriptive purposes. In calculating rough estimates of the economic returns from marriage, however, I employ an expected value model, and so I use the mean instead of the median.

The expected income of the husband of a female university graduate is calculated as follows:

Table 4B.1: Association between husband's and wife's educational levels

a. For male respondents

Husband (Respondent)	Wife (Spouse) (%)				
	University	Junior college/ technical college	Senior high school	Junior high school	(N)
University	24	29	45	3	(501)
Junior college/technical college	3	22	70	5	(37)
Senior high school	2	8	75	15	(920)
Junior high school	0	1	30	69	(519)

$\gamma = .841$, $\tau_c = .502$

b. For female respondents

Husband (Spouse) (%)	Wife (Respondent)			
	University	Junior college/ technical college	Senior high school	Junior high school
University	83	59	21	4
Junior college/technical college	2	6	4	1
Senior high school	12	33	62	29
Junior high school	2	2	14	66
(N)	(164)	(273)	(1312)	(646)

$\gamma = .799$, $\tau_c = .477$

Note: These tables show the educational levels of respondents' spouse in the current or recent marriage, including cases of divorce or spousal death. A technical college (*kōtō-senmon-gakkō* or '*kōsen*') is a five-year school for junior-high-school graduates, which awards its graduands a degree equivalent to a junior-college degree. Educational levels before the Educational Reform of 1947 are coded as the corresponding levels after the Reform.

Data: Social Stratification and Social Mobility Survey (SSM Survey) in Japan, 1995, Questionnaires A and B.

$$E \text{ (University)} = 0.83 \times 8,200 + 0.02 \times 10,500 + 0.12 \times 7,180 + 0.02 \times 5,500$$
$$= 7,987.6 \text{ (thousand yen)}.$$

Similarly, the expected values of a husband's income for women who graduated from a junior college/technical college, a senior- or a junior high school are, respectively:

E (Junior college/technical college) = 6,640.1 (thousand yen),

Figure 4B.1: Wife's and husband's educational levels and husband's mean income (including tax)

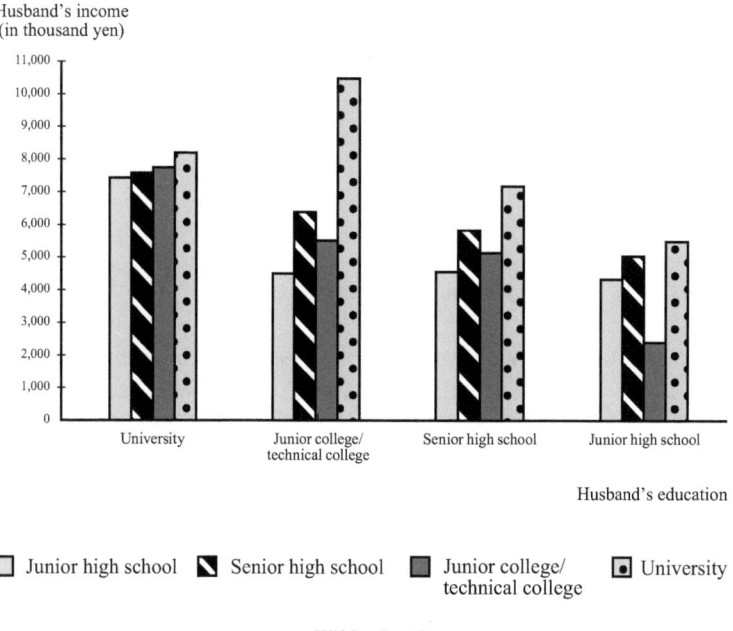

Note: Respondents are wives aged under 60; excluding cases of divorce and husband's death. Educational levels before the Educational Reform of 1947 are coded as the corresponding levels after the Reform.
Data: Social Stratification and Social Mobility Survey (SSM Survey) in Japan, 1995, Questionnaires A and B.

E (Senior high school) = 6,173.1 (thousand yen),
and
E (Junior high school) = 4,510.0 (thousand yen).

(We may round these estimates to the nearest ten thousand yen, that is, write these estimates to three significant figures.) The economic return of education through marriage for a Japanese woman thus seems to increase as her educational level rises. As these figures are only rough estimates, however, we should take into account the age effect, cohort effect and period effect, for a more accurate estimation.

5 Job Discontinuation and Return to the Workforce after First Childbirth: The Case of Young Married Korean Women

Jikyung Kim

Women's labour participation in Korea

Discussions on female labour from the 1990s to the present have been focused on underutilisation. The utilisation of female labour has been a big issue because Korea needs human resources to continue economic growth and maintain economic and social welfare. As Korean society is entering an age of low births and rapid ageing, the dependent population will become larger than the working population in the future. In this situation, the active use of underutilised females could be a solution to the envisaged shortage in the working-age population. During the last thirty years, the total fertility rate in Korea plunged from 4.5 children per reproductive woman in 1970 to 1.2 in 2003. On the other hand, the ageing rate rose steadily from 5.8 per cent in 1980 to 9.1 per cent in 2000. In present Korean society, the population aged sixty-five or older is over seven per cent of the whole population, suggesting that Korea is indeed an ageing society.

Since industrialisation, female labour in Korea has not only undergone an expansion in volume from 36.0 per cent in 1963 to 49.8 per cent in 2004, but also has experienced qualitative evolution, from being composed of poorly-schooled young women engaged in simple labour to comprising a female workforce which is highly-schooled and able to do specialised labour. Despite this quantitative and qualitative growth of female labour, however, women's labour-force participation rate is still below fifty per cent, the underutilisation of female labour mainly being due to the interruption in women's work-career during their late twenties and early thirties because of childbirth and child-rearing.

Figure 5.1, which was published by the ILO, compares the women's labour-force participation rate by age among the United States, Japan, Germany, Korea and Norway. As shown in that figure, the labour-force

Figure 5.1: Women's economic activity rate

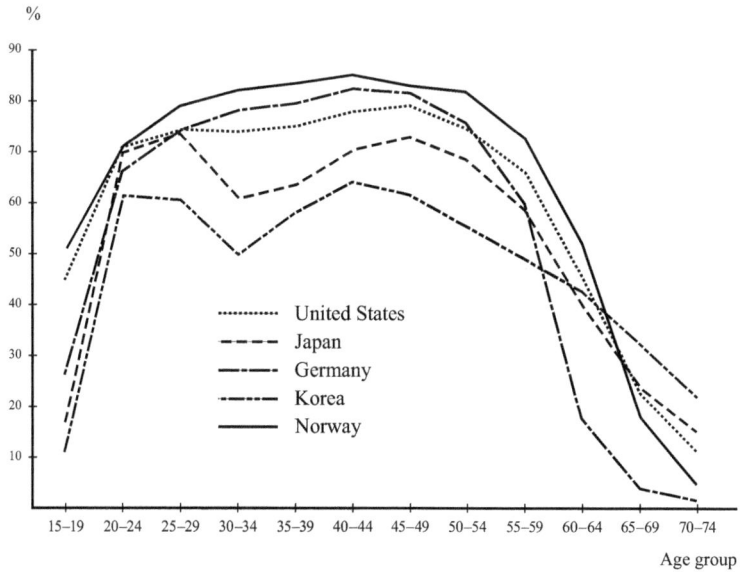

Source: *ILO Year Book of Labour Statistics* 2004

structure in Korea and Japan is M-shaped. This structure disappeared in Western developed countries in the 1980s. According to an OECD report in 2002, the labour-force participation rate drops significantly during the age of childbirth and child-rearing, rebounds in women's early forties and falls again in their mid- and late forties. Among OECD countries, the two-peak structure is found only in Korea and Japan. This shows that in Korea and Japan, despite the steady rise in the women's labour-force participation rate, the rate by age still remains that of an M-shaped structure due to the interruption in work career for childbirth and child-rearing.

Figure 5.2 indicates the Korean women's labour-force participation rate by age in 1980, 1990, 2000 and 2004. At a glance, it can be seen that the decrease in the labour-force participation rate during women's late twenties and their early thirties grew smaller between 1980 and 2004. However, only the age corresponding to the lowest rate moved from 25–29 to 30–34. The M-shaped labour-force structure was not resolved. The movement in the age of the lowest rate resulted from a delayed age of marriage. For example, the age of women's first marriage was twenty-three in 1980 but was deferred for 4.5 years to 27.5 in 2004.

Figure 5.2: Korean women's labour-force participation rate by age

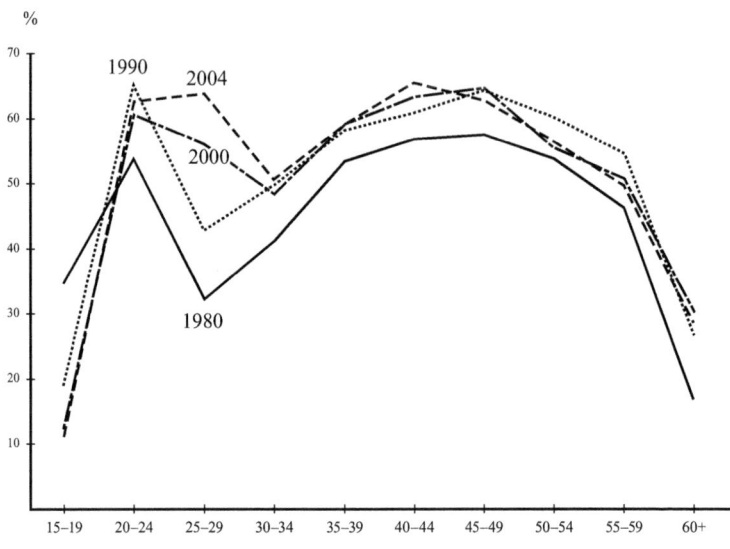

Source: *Annual Report on the Economically Active Population Survey of Korea*, National Statistical Office 2005

Interruption in work career due to childbirth and child-rearing breaks the learning curve and wastes human resources and, because of these factors, women suffer discrimination in employment, promotion, education and wages. As a result, they look for a job lower than their qualifications or even give up entering the labour market altogether. This aggravates the distinctions between men and women in terms of occupational type and position and solidifies the gender-inequality structure. In other words, interruption in career-life solidifies the gendered distinction between occupations; limits women's employment opportunities to low-waged and low-skilled jobs, thus producing a large volume of highly-schooled but idle human resources; and polarises the internal structure of the female labour market.

Women who have been continuously employed in the labour market will have highly-skilled and highly-waged jobs, while, on the contrary, those who have experienced interruption in their work career and have then come back to the labour market are likely to have low-skilled and low-waged jobs. In this way, interruption in work career creates a female labour market which is double-layered and divided into two heterogeneous groups:

> Childbirth /Child-rearing → Distinction of occupational type; limitation in employment opportunities → Low wage and low skill → Mass production of idle human resources → Polarisation of the female labour market

In order to solve the problem of the underutilisation of female labour, we need to investigate the pattern of interruption in work career due to childbirth and subsequent child-rearing, to examine who returns to the labour market and who remains unemployed, and to identify factors determining women's return to the labour market. The aim of this chapter, therefore, is to survey the length of interruption in women's work career after their first birth; to analyse factors determining their return to the labour market; and to provide basic information for policy-making on the utilisation of female labour to fill the expected future shortage in the working-age population.

Theories on women's labour-market participation

Two representative theories on women's labour market participation are the 'economic theory' and the 'feminist theory,' the latter being one which criticises the fundamental assumptions of the economic approach and focuses on gender roles. The neoclassical economic theory on married women's participation in the labour market takes the view that, under the limitations of time and budget, change in the market wage affects individuals' choice, and the supply of labour is determined by comparison between the reservation wage and the market wage. The reservation wage means benefits which would be given up or time and financial costs a worker would incur by participating in the labour market. That is, if the market wage earned through employment is smaller than the reservation wage, women will tend not to work in the labour market, but if the wage proposed by the market is larger than or at least the same as the reservation wage, then married women may participate in the labour market.

Expanding the basic model above, Mincer (1960) explained that the choice of labour supply is not a matter of choice between working in the labour market and having free time, but a matter of distribution among three choices: working in the labour market; working at home; and having free time. In addition, he extended the existing model, which assumed the limitations of time and budget, with the idea that decision-making vis-à-vis labour supply is affected not only by the wage earned in the market but also by household income.

Following Mincer (1960), Becker (1965) explained married women's labour supply with a theory called the household production function model. He assumed that married women's labour supply is determined by the time-distribution among market labour, pure leisure and various non-market activities. Differing from previous views, the household production model emphasised that the household is not simply a consumer but a producer—manufacturing commodities and services by putting in time and household labour. According to that theory, individuals do productive work not only in the market but also at home and decide whether to participate in the labour market after comparing productivity in the market with that at home.

Married women's reservation wage is higher when their children are young and the number of children is large (Nakamura and Nakamura 1991). This is because, unlike other types of housework, child-rearing cannot easily be replaced with a market product. In addition, even if child-rearing services can be provided in the market, married women must pay that price in order to work in the labour market. In general, the net market wage of women with children is their wage after deducting the expense of child-rearing and, as a result, their income decreases and the reservation wage increases with the birth of children (Heckman 1974; Blau and Robins 1988; Klerman and Leibowitz 1990; Connelly 1992).

In this way, the neoclassical economic explanation questions neither the characteristics of female labour that participates in the labour market discontinuously due to pregnancy, childbirth and child-rearing, nor the structure of the labour market which is discriminatory against women, both until and after they enter the market. Rather, it regards the withdrawal of female labour from the labour market resulting from marriage, pregnancy, childbirth and child-rearing as a rational action chosen by each individual of her own accord and as a condition or premise given to the gender-discriminatory labour market. However, women are more likely to quit their jobs because of fixed social ideas or ideologies on gender roles, including various social pressures which occur when women postpone marriage or neglect child-rearing and housework for their vocational achievements rather than by their own choice.

In order to supplement the limitations of the neoclassical theory on female labour, the statistical discrimination theory was developed in consideration of the demand for a labour force. In this theory, statistical discrimination means discrimination caused by employers' imperfect information about the labour market or labour suppliers. In general, companies have uncertain information about individuals, and the collection of information costs a huge amount. Therefore, individuals' capabilities and their labour quality have to be assessed based on the average properties of the group to which the individuals belong. Thus, employers with limited information pursue high profits by excluding women (who are highly likely to stop working midterm) from jobs which require a high cost in replacement or training (Bielby and Baron 1986). In addition, it is optimistically projected that if these assumptions about women quitting their jobs are found to be incorrect and unreasonable, then such employers' discrimination will disappear over time.

Another theory that approaches from the aspect of labour demand is the dual labour market theory, which is a kind of labour market segmentation theory. According to the labour market segmentation theory, the labour market and the economic system are divided into two or more segments, which differ from one another in quality. That is, labourers belonging to different segments work under different labour conditions, preferences and structures and these differences come not from difference in the workers' personal characteristics but from the structure of the economic system or the labour market. Based on the contents of the labour market segmentation theory, the dual labour market theory explains that the labour market is divided into the primary and secondary labour markets, respectively, depending on the employment structure and the wage structure of the labour market. That is, the primary labour market guarantees high wages, a stable employment state, and diverse opportunities for internal promotion, while the secondary labour market is characterised by unstable employment caused by low wages and poor working conditions. The major difference between the primary labour market and the secondary labour market is found in the relative stability of employment. Movement between these segmented labour markets is limited. Major criteria for the segmentation of the labour market are gender, educational level, job category, wage level and employment type, and both academic qualifications and gender, especially, are important influential factors in the case of the Korean labour market.

In general, while the male labour force is supplied by the primary labour market, the female one is supplied by the secondary labour market. For the reason that women are deemed not suitable for primary job categories which generally demand stable and continuous employment, they are shut off from the primary labour market which guarantees high wages and promotion, and so are pushed to the secondary market. This theory explains that even if the characteristics of female human capital change, there will be scant improvement in women's status until the market is restructured or a larger number of women get jobs in the primary market.

In contrast to the economic viewpoint, the feminist viewpoint thinks it is insufficient to explain women's participation in the labour market only in terms of economic demand and supply, and turns its eye instead to how the patriarchal structure works in the labour market and discriminates against female labour.

Early feminist researchers who studied female labour explained problems in the female labour market in terms of 'industrial reserve forces' in the relation between capital and labour. Industrial reserve forces mean reserve labour forces that can flow in or out of the labour market as occasion demands. They are cheap labour forces which come into the labour market during boom-times and go back home during recession periods. One of the important grounds for women to be regarded as industrial reserve forces is gender specialisation ideology which views women's role as that of taking charge of household labour and child-rearing at home. This is still a valid explanation in contemporary society where women are widely utilised as part-time labourers. However, early feminists' discussions based on the Marxist analytic frame overemphasise the relation between capital and labour and, as a consequence, this theory has limitations in explaining the phenomenon of men's domination of women, as observed in various groups in the labour market.

It was the theory of patriarchal capitalism that was raised in order to supplement the limitations of early feminist theory. In the later theory, the patriarchal system is defined as men's control over the female labour force. Because the patriarchal system preceded the occurrence of capitalism, the patriarchal relation in employment cannot be understood in terms of capitalism alone. Gendered job-segregation found in the labour market is the effect of the patriarchal system on the labour market, and is regarded as the primary mechanism which maintains men's dominance over women in capitalist society. As a result of gendered job-segregation, unmarried women who receive a low wage become dependent on men through marriage, and it is taken for granted that married women will take full charge of household labour for their husbands. It is explained that men benefit from traditional gender-specialisation in both wage labour and household labour. This theory of patriarchal capitalism insists that it is necessary to focus on the effects of the patriarchal system and women's gender roles and responsibility, as well as on how men protect their vested rights in the labour market and at home. Furthermore, it raises the fundamental question of whether the economic concepts and theories used in research on the female labour market are effective in explaining women's labour experiences. That is, it asserts the necessity of new concepts and theories reflecting women's experiences and their particular conditions.

Women's employment patterns after childbirth

Generally, the influence of childbirth on women's employment has been found to be negative in previous research (Becker 1965; Heckman 1974; Blau and Robin 1989; Klerman and Leibowiz 1990; Connelly 1992; Lee 1996, Kim 1998, Park 2002). This is because childbirth demands women's time and effort, and working after childbirth requires labour-supply costs including child-rearing expenses, which in turn reduces women's net market wage and brings a negative influence to bear upon women's employment. As shown in the distribution of Korean women's economic activity participation rate, their participation in economic activity is low during the period around childbirth due to the influence of childbirth on women's employment, and is relatively high after completion of childbirth and child-rearing. This shows that women's employability is closely linked to the event of childbirth.

After childbirth, a woman's employment status may be one of continuous employment, new employment, or change from employment to unemployment. A representative study on the pattern of change in women's employment status after childbirth was made by Hakim (1996), who analysed English women's movements in the labour market by using data from the WES (Women and Employment Survey). In her research, Hakim (1996) classified women's employment-life patterns into three types: continuous employment; career homemaking which involves withdrawal from the labour market due to marriage or childbirth; and discontinuous employment with cycles of employment and unemployment.

According to the result of Hakim's analysis, in younger generations, the percentage of discontinuous employment (forty-eight per cent) is higher than that of continuous employment (fifteen per cent) or homemaker (thirty-seven per cent), and while the increase in continuous employment was insignificant, the change from homemaker to discontinuous employment was significant. Based on the result, Hakim concluded that although the total female labour force in the market had increased, a large number of women showed discontinuous employment because their working period was not continuous, but broken up throughout their life-cycle.

With regard to this subject, there is only one piece of research (Kim 1998) that has analysed data from the Korean Women's Development Institute on the current state of women's employment. According to the results of the research, employment patterns observed in Korean married women were, in order: discontinuous employment (32.8 per cent); homemaking in which women stopped working after marriage (28.0 per cent); employment after marriage (16.7 per cent); continuous employment (11.4 per cent); and unemployment (11.1 per cent). Moreover, the continuous-employment group was quite heterogeneous, containing a high percentage of those with low academic qualifications as well as those with high academic qualifications, and the employment-after-marriage group was characterised by low academic qualifications and high age.

Another fact found in these two bodies of research is that the continuity of employment appears differently according to job category. Movements are infrequent and the continuity of employment in the same job is long in professional jobs demanding high-level education and training, but not in job categories such as manufacturing or sales and service. In the case of Korean married women, movements among job categories take place mostly in a vertical downward direction (Kim, 1998), showing that childbirth and child-rearing are the major causes of labour interruption and the costs are high in terms of women's employment and career opportunities.

According to the patterns of married women's employment states after childbirth classified by Hakim (1996) and Kim (1998), a large percentage of those in continuous employment has high academic qualifications as well as professional jobs. These types of women include those who withdraw from the labour market temporarily during maternity leave and come back to the market within two months from childbirth, as opposed to those who come back to the labour market but after an interval of more than two months from childbirth.

Secondly, there are those homemakers who are in employment before childbirth but withdraw from the labour market and join the non-economically-active population after childbirth. In Korea, college graduates have been known to belong typically to the group of homemakers. According to the results of recent research (Kim, 1998), however, the percentage of high-school graduates appears high in this group. This suggests that, with the rise in women's academic qualifications, high-school graduates who have been employed mainly as simple office workers have difficulty in maintaining their jobs or re-entering into the labour market after childbirth. On the other hand, this shows that while married women with a Bachelor's degree do not supply labour of their own accord, it is growing more difficult for high-school graduates to maintain their jobs and re-enter the labour market because of the structural problems of the labour market.

Thirdly, there are those groups in discontinuous employment which, according to Hakim's report, is observed frequently in young women who are in employment before childbirth, withdraw from the labour market during the period of child-rearing following birth, and then return to the market after the end of the child-rearing period. In Korea, this group is known to include mainly those of low academic qualifications and older age. This is typical among those who are in economic demand at home or among those who experience a great deal of occupational change in the labour market.

The patterns in employment state after childbirth as discussed above are determined by whether married women who had been in employment before childbirth return to the labour market after having their child. Accordingly, the factors which determine employment status after childbirth can be explained in the same context as the factors which induce married women to return to the labour market after childbirth.

Factors influencing employment status after childbirth

Among research which has analysed women's entrance into and withdrawal from the labour market around childbirth, some studies report that women are returning to the labour market after childbirth sooner, yet there are other reports that many women are not very likely to come back to the labour market at all.

Desai and Waite (1991), who reported the early return of married women to the labour market, said that there is a gradual tendency for women to minimise their career interruption by withdrawing from the labour market as late as possible before childbirth and re-entering the market as early as possible. Dex and Joshi (1999), who examined changes in the English women's labour-market participation rate, agreed with this opinion and said that a major reason for the increase in women's economic activity participation rate is their return to the labour market after having taken only a short period of leave after childbirth. Supporting these views, Garret et al. (1990) analysed data from the NLSY (National Longitudinal Survey of Youth) in the United States and showed that seventy-three per cent of women who had been employed before pregnancy return to their work within one year after childbirth. A different opinion is offered by Even (1987), who, through his analysis on career interruption after childbirth, reported that most respondents show an L-shaped distribution, which suggests a low possibility for many women to return to the labour market.

With a review of the previous research as above, we will now examine factors which affect married women's return to the labour market with the shortest career interruption caused by childbirth, by dividing them into five categories: demographic characteristics; human resources; family and child-rearing; household economic conditions; and the market environment.

Demographic characteristics
Demographic characteristics to be considered are age, academic qualifications and the birth of a second child. Excluding academic qualifications, which will be discussed under the characteristics of human resources, here we discuss age and the interval between childbirths. According to previous research, younger women are known to return to the labour market earlier than older women. For example, according to Desai and Waite (1991), young women are more likely to re-enter the labour market after childbirth and have a stronger desire for employment.

According to Phang (1994), who analysed American women using NLSY data, however, young women are more likely to move from unemployment to employment but, at the same time, to move from employment to unemployment. Therefore, in the case of young women, their employment is not continuous, but, as was reported by Hakim (1996), their participation in the labour market is distributed intermittently throughout their lives.

On the other hand, Klerman and Leibowitz (1994) said that there is an earlier return to the labour market when the childbirth is not the woman's first, and Lee (1996) reported that the transition rate to participation in the labour market after the birth of the last child is 2.8 times higher than that before marriage. In this way, re-entry into the labour market is quicker though withdrawal from the market is frequent among young women, and, particularly when the child is not the first, the mother's period of career interruption is shorter and her return to work sooner if she is young.

Factors related to human resources
In re-entry into and withdrawal from the labour market around childbirth, the most important factor related to human resources is women's wage based on academic qualifications and work experience. As for the effects of academic qualifications during the period around childbirth, and particularly in the process of withdrawal from and return to the labour market, the results of previous research are not clear, and this can be explained in the same context as the fact that, as discussed above, the mechanism of labour-supply decision-making in a married woman's life is a very complex one.

With regard to the opinion that those with high academic qualifications are more likely to experience interruption in employment and then return to the labour market, Chang (1997) held the view that highly-educated women tend to attach much importance to child-rearing. Their wage-demand becomes higher after childbirth and, as a consequence, their high academic qualifications have a negative effect on their participation in the labour market after childbirth. Contrary to this view, Leibowitz et al. (1991) maintained that, rather than high academic qualifications, it is low qualifications—high school or below—which have a negative effect on women's return to the labour market, and Klerman and Leibowitz (1994) also reported a result which contrasted with that of Chang (1997), saying that highly-educated women are less likely to leave the labour market during their pregnancy. On the other hand, Flemlee (1984) said that women of high educational level leave the labour market early because they can re-enter the market with comparative ease. This shows that, relatively speaking, highly-educated women are freer to enter and withdraw from the labour market than less-educated women.

Previous researchers who analysed the effects of academic qualifications on re-entry to the labour market also produced conflicting results. Klerman and Leibowitz (1990) reported that academic qualifications have a positive effect on women's return to the labour market after childbirth and highly-educated women who expect high wages tend to return to their job early after childbirth.

Conversely, Greenstein (1989) reported that academic qualifications have a negative effect on women's return to the labour market after childbirth. In the research by Lee (1996), as well, the transition rate from unemployment to employment was low in women who were college graduates. This shows that Korean women with a Bachelor's degree or higher academic qualifications have a long period of unemployment once they become unemployed. In Kim's (1998) research, however, it was found that high-school graduates have a longer period of unemployment than college graduates.

With regard to work experience which, together with academic qualifications, is reflected in wages, most of the previous research supports the opinion that those with long work experience are less likely to have career interruption and are more easily able to return to the labour market. Park (2001) reported that women who experience marriage and childbirth before their first period of employment defer their employment for over eight years compared to those who do not, and those who experience marriage and childbirth after their first period of employment maintain their employment status for a specific period and withdraw from the labour market when having a second child.

Kim (1998) reported that past experience in the labour market has a huge effect. That is, for each transition between employment and unemployment in the past, a woman's transition rate to employment increases by around 1.2 times and, in this way, women who have frequent entrances into and withdrawals from the labour market can re-enter the labour market more easily than those who do not, and those with a longer period of unemployment have more difficulty in getting a job.

According to Chang (1997), work experience has a stronger effect than academic qualifications, and longer work experience lowers the possibility of withdrawal from the labour market. Moreover, according to Barrow (1999), around seventy-five per cent of those who have worked before their first childbirth return to the labour market within a year.

What is notable, however, is that the effect of work experience in the labour market varies depending on the existence of children. According to Flemlee (1984), voluntary withdrawal from the labour market decreases with an increase in the length of service but increases when there are children. This suggests that factors related to children are more influential on married women's labour supply than factors related to human resources such as work experience.

Together with factors related to children, a wage which reflects academic qualifications and work experience is another important factor determining women's participation in the labour market. As is well-known, women receiving a high wage in the market are less likely to move from employment to unemployment. Mason and Kuhlthau (1992) considered that women's wage levels are more important than the income level of other family members, including the husband, and employment was less affected by child-rearing in highly-paid women than in low-paid women. Wenk and Garret (1992) also reported that the negative effect of the husband's income on women's continuous employment after childbirth decreases gradually and that women's income gains a relatively strong effect from it.

According to the research of Klerman and Leibowitz (1990), the period for returning to the labour market varies depending on the wage level which women receive in the market—those women who obtained a high market wage returning to the labour market within three months after childbirth. It is also reported that a high wage in the market lowers the transition rate from employment to unemployment, not only after childbirth, but also during pregnancy before childbirth (Flemlee 1984). After all, because early return to the labour market after childbirth can narrow the gap between women's potential wage and their real wage (Barrow 1999; Johnes 1999), those who receive a high wage tend to return to the labour market earlier.

On the other hand, Dex et al. (1998) have said that women with a high wage who have deferred childbirth tend to work in the market while their children are young. According to Dex et al., women who are in their early twenties and have children show as high a labour-market participation rate as highly-paid women who defer childbirth, but the former's period of employment is not always continuous. On the other hand, Dex et al. assert that low-waged women have few opportunities for employment, regardless of whether they defer childbirth.

Factors related to family and child-rearing
Child-rearing, which is least substitutable with services provided in the market, is one of the direct factors which bring career interruption to women. It is already well-known that women who have a child-carer are highly likely to work (Lerer and Nerlove 1984; Clifford and Tobin 1977). Klerman and Leibowitz (1990), for example, showed that women with a relative who can provide childcare service return to the labour market early after childbirth and around half of the women who have returned to the labour market within three months have a

relative in charge of child-rearing. To young children, being reared by a relative is as valuable as being reared by their own parents; and the presence of relatives makes women less conscious of the limitations of labour-supply and releases them from the burden of child-rearing (Mason and Kuhlthau, 1992).

According to Sung and Chah (2002), a woman's cohabitation with member(s) of her parents' generation who can take care of her children—particularly female elders—has a positive effect on the woman's working hours because female elders can provide a married working woman with resources related to housework and child-rearing. In general, high expenses for child-rearing force women to withdraw from the labour market (Blau and Robin 1989; Connelly 1992, Barrow 1999). Thus, women with relatives who can take charge of children spend less money on child-rearing than those without such relations (Heckman 1974), or else they have a relatively low reservation wage, so they are more positive towards the labour supply.

Factors related to the household economy
Because the level of household income means the power to purchase spare time, high income increases the possibility that market labour will be replaced with household labour or spare time. In particular, married women are more likely than men to decide their participation in economic activities according to the income of their spouses or other family members (Chang and Kim 2001). In general, the total household income apart from the married women's earned income has a negative effect on married women's participation in the labour market and their working hours. This supports the theory of income effect that women supply labour for livelihood or for helping family finances.

According to Klerman and Leibowitz (1990), women tend to return to the labour market soon after childbirth when their husband's income is low, but are less likely to work and tend to move from employment to unemployment if their family has a large amount of assets and high income from their husband or other family members. In research by Dex et al. (1998), as well, the husband's income appeared to have a negative effect on women's return to the labour market after childbirth. According to Wenk and Garrett (1992), in younger generations, the effect of women's own income on their participation in the labour market after childbirth increases and the effect of their husband's income decreases.

In this way, factors related to the household economy such as the husband's income and the total household income still have a negative effect on women's labour supply and, in particular, their return to the labour market after childbirth, but, as shown by recent research, women's own market wage has a stronger effect than household economy variables in explaining their labour market behaviour. This suggests that married women's labour supply is going beyond the level of subsidiary labour supply just to help family finances.

Factors related to the market environment

Factors to be considered in relation to the labour market environment are the economic and institutional characteristics of the area of women's residence. First, among the economic characteristics of the area of residence, the unemployment rate was found to have a significant effect on women's return to the labour market (Barrow 1999). Women residing in a large city are less likely to live together with their parents, so those with young children have difficulty in finding a helper for child-rearing, and this exerts a negative effect upon married women's working hours (Sung and Chah 2002).

With regard to institutional characteristics, tax deduction from gross income for child-rearing expenses increases net income, so it stimulates return to the labour market. Accordingly, tax deduction from income is an important determinant for women's return to the labour market (Klerman and Leibowitz 1990).

However, according to Leibowitz et al. (1991), the deduction of a large amount of child-rearing expenses from income increases women's return to the labour market within three months of childbirth, but has little effect on women's labour supply three or more months after childbirth. Ultimately, the deduction of child-rearing expenses from income seems to be very effective in promoting early return to the labour market after childbirth, but not to be very effective in the long run.

Empirical analysis on job discontinuation and return

Analysed data and respondents

Data analysed in this study comprised work-history data from 1998 to 2001 surveyed by the Korea Labor and Income Panel Study (hereinafter KLIPS) which captured the process of labour-market transition for people from the age of fifteen, up to the year 2001. The KLIPS data is longitudinal data acquired annually since 1998 which evaluates the economic activities, labour-market transfers, income, consumption, education, vocational training and social life of respondents who represent Korean households in non-rural areas (KLI 2002). The work-history data was accumulated through repetitive surveys over four years. This data includes retrospective data which contains information on all jobs experienced by the sample household members aged fifteen or older.

The respondents were 128 married women who had children, had been employed in the past, had given birth to their first child after 1997, and had been in employment before childbirth. The reason for limiting the scope of research to these women was that the KLIPS data did not include information on childbirth, et cetera, before 1997, except for some retrospective data related to labour-market work experience.

The details of the respondents are as follows: In Figure 5.3, the two vertical lines indicate the year 1997 and the year 2001, respectively. The year 1997 is the base-line used to select women who gave birth to children after that point in time, and the year 2001 is the end of the observation period. Woman 'A' gave birth to a child before 1997 and returned to the labour market after 1997, so she is not included in the analysis of this research. 'B' and 'C' gave birth to a child after 1997 and returned to the labour market before the end of the observation period, so they are included in the analysis. 'D' gave birth to a child after 1997 but did not return to the labour market before the end of the period of observation, so she is included in the analysis as a right-censored case. 'E' gave birth to a child just before the end of the observation period and was on maternity leave until the end of the observation, so she, too, is included in the analysis as a right-censored case, like 'D'. 'F' gave birth to a child before 1997 and did not return to the labour market before the end of the observation period, so she is not included in the analysis. 'G' had never given birth to a child in her lifetime, so she is not included in the analysis, either. Accordingly, the respondents included in the analysis for this study are B, C, D and E.

Analysis model and variables

In order to identify factors influencing women's return to the labour market after childbirth, we selected Cox's proportional-hazards model. The model is called 'survival analysis' in medicine, 'event history analysis' in sociology and 'duration analysis' in economics. This method is useful in analysing the duration from the point of entering into a specific state until withdrawal from that state, namely, the time interval, spell, duration or waiting time. By including censored data, this method can reduce sample-selection bias and minimise data loss.

Figure 5.3: The analysed respondents

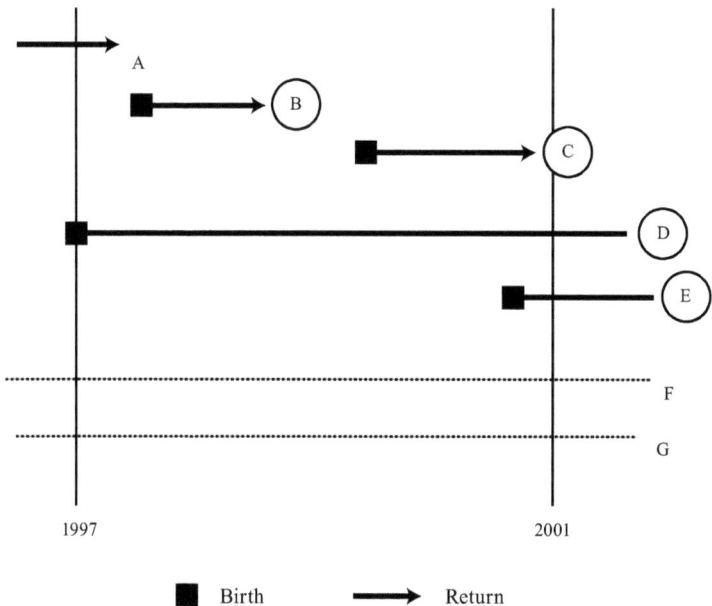

While Cox's model is focused on duration, logistic regression is focused on whether a specific event has happened. For example, we can do logistic regression analysis with the data of survival analysis by dividing respondents according to whether a specific event has happened, based on a specific point in time. However, if the follow-up period is short or the number of events too small, compared to the size of the data, then estimated regressions can be similar. However, if the percentage of censored data is high, values estimated through logistic regression analysis will have bias.

In the analysis model of this research, childbirth is the beginning of the period in question, and return to the labour market is the event of withdrawal from the period, the duration between these two points in time comprising the analysis unit. The duration (or spell) from the time of childbirth to the time of return to the labour market as the unit of analysis is followed by the hazard function following $h_i(t)$:

$$h_i(t) = h_0(t) \exp(Z'_i \beta)$$
$$= h_0(t) \exp(\beta_1 z_{i1} + \beta_2 z_{i12} + \cdots + \beta_p z_{ip})$$

Here, the '$h_0(t)$' is a baseline hazard function. The 'Z'_i' is the vector of independent variables and the 'β' represents the regression parameters of independent variables. This model is estimated by the partial likelihood method. The dependent variable is the cumulative hazard function, which is the percentage of women who return to the labour market in a specific time after childbirth, as shown in Figure 5.4—that is, the hazard rate of the event of return to the labour market after childbirth.

Independent variables include age at childbirth, academic qualifications, husband's average monthly income, the decision whether to have a child-carer after childbirth and before returning to the labour market, type of employment before childbirth, type of working hours, occupation, earned income and length of service.

Figure 5.4: The analysed unit

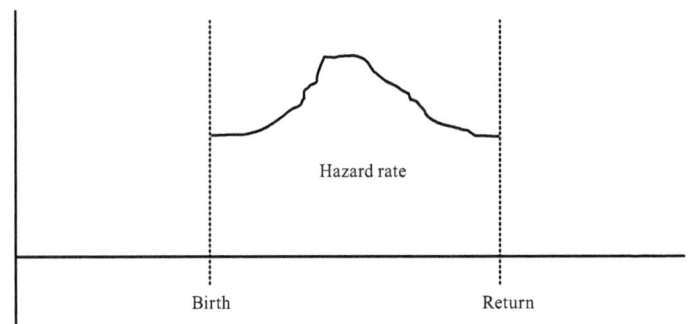

Table 5.1: Definitions and measuring methods of variables

Variable	Definition and measuring method		
Dependent variables	Hazard rate during the period from childbirth to return to the labour market		
Explanatory variables			
Categorical			
Academic qualification	Two-year college and above	1 = Yes	0 = No
Child-carer	One who takes care of children	1 = Existing	0 = Not existing
Type of employment	Type of employment	1 = Waged	0 = Non-waged
Type of working hours	Type of working hours	1 = Full-time	0 = Part-time
Occupation	Specialist or manager	1 = Yes	0 = No
Continuous			
Age	Age		
Husband's income	Natural log of husband's average monthly income		
Earned income	Natural log of average monthly wage at the job before childbirth		
Length of service	Total length of service at the workplace before childbirth		

Table 5.2: Characteristics of respondents

Variable	Value	Number of cases	Percentage/ average	Standard deviation
Demographic characteristics				
Age	Less than 30	105	82.0	
	Over 30	23	18.0	
	Average (years)		27.2	3.1
Academic qualification	High school and below	75	58.6	
	Two-year college	25	19.5	
	Four-year college and above	28	21.9	
	Average (years)		13.3	1.9
Household characteristics				
Child-carer	Existing	33	25.8	
	Not existing	95	74.2	
Husband's income	Husband's average monthly income (won[a])		1,426,000	1,013,000
Occupational characteristics before childbirth				
Type of employment	Waged work	109	85.2	
	Non-waged work	19	14.8	
Type of occupation	Specialist or manager	31	24.2	
	Office worker	54	42.2	
	Service worker	28	21.8	
	Manufacturing worker	7	5.5	
Type of work time	Full-time	84	65.6	
	Part-time	44	34.4	
Earned income	Average monthly wage (won)		949,000	476,000
Length of service	Length of service (months)		49.4	37.9

a: 1 US dollar = 930 Korean Won

Table 5.1 shows the definitions of variables and how to measure them, while Table 5.2 shows the general characteristics of the respondents.

The results of analysis

Duration until return to the labour market after childbirth

Table 5.3 shows changes in employment status from childbirth. According to the table, 54.7 per cent of the respondents returned to the labour market after childbirth and maintained their job, and it took 8.6 months postpartum, on the average, for them to return to the labour market. Table 5.4, on the other hand, shows the patterns

Table 5.3: Duration from childbirth to return to the labour market and change in employment status (N = 128, Ratio = 100.0)

	Whether respondents returned to the labour market after childbirth		Average duration until return (months)
	Number of cases	Percentage	
Returned	70	54.7	8.6
Not returned	58	45.3	–

of the average career-interruption period according to individual characteristics. First, by age, the average career-interruption period was 10.2 months in women younger than thirty years, and 4.0 months in those at thirty or older, so the former period was around 2.5 times longer than the latter.

By academic qualifications, the average interruption period was shorter in women with higher academic qualifications. It was 12.1 months in high-school graduates or below and 6.3 months in two-year college graduates. On the other hand, university graduates (who had studied for four or more years at tertiary level) showed the shortest interruption period (5.5 months). In this way, the average interruption period in high-school graduates was more than two times longer than that of college graduates, showing a large difference according to academic qualifications, though the respondents of analysis were young women of similar age.

As to whether married women had a helper to take charge of child-rearing so that those women could return to the labour market, the average career-interruption period was three months in those with such a helper, which was around one fourth of the interruption period in those without (12.1 months). What is more, based on the husband's average monthly earned income, which is an indicator of family economic status, the average career-interruption period was 9.0 months and 8.2 months, respectively, in women whose husband's average monthly income was below 1,000,000 won (US$1=930 Korean won), and between 1,000,000 and 2,000,000 won. On the other hand, women whose husband's average monthly income was over 2,000,000 won had an average interruption period of 9.6 months, which was somewhat longer than that of the previous two groups.

As discussed above, in terms of demographic characteristics and family economy, the career-interruption period resulting from childbirth was shortest in married women who were aged thirty years or older; and who were college graduates; and who had a helper to rear

Table 5.4: *Duration of job discontinuation according to demographic and household characteristics (N = 70, Ratio = 100.0)*

Characteristic		No. of cases	%	Average duration of job discontinuation (months)	Standard deviation
Demographic characteristics					
Age	Less than 30	52	74.3	10.2	12.4
	Over 30	18	25.7	4.0	8.5
Academic qualifications	High school and below	31	44.3	12.1	14.2
	Two-year college	17	24.3	6.3	9.7
	Four-year college and above	22	31.4	5.5	8.0
Household characteristics					
Child-carer	Existing	43	61.4	3.0	3.7
	Not existing	27	38.6	12.1	13.6
Husband's income (won[a])	Under 1,000,000	15	21.4	9.0	11.1
	1,000,000–2,000,000	43	61.4	8.2	11.8
	Over 2,000,000	12	17.2	9.6	13.3

a: 1 US dollar = 930 Korean Won

children for them; and whose husband's average monthly income was between 1,000,000 and 2,000,000 won.

Table 5.5 shows the career-interruption period according to the type of job before childbirth. First, by the type of employment, the career-interruption period was 3.6 months longer in women employed in non-waged labour before childbirth than in those employed in waged labour; and, by working hours, the duration of non-employment was 14.5 months in women who had been part-time workers, which was over three times longer than the 4.2 months in women who had been full-time workers. In addition, according to job category, the average interruption period was longest (17.3 months) in women who had been manufacturing workers before childbirth and shortest (6.2 months) in those who had been office workers. According to earned income from their job, the career-interruption period was longest (12.8 months) in women whose average monthly income was between 500,000 and 1,000,000 won, and shortest (4.1 months) in women with earned income below 500,000 won. According to length of service, the career-interruption period was around four times longer in women who had worked for less than five years than in those who had worked for more than five years.

Table 5.5: Duration of job discontinuation according to occupational characteristics (N=70, Ratio=100.0)

Occupational characteristic before childbirth		No. of cases	%	Average duration of job discontinuation (months)	Standard deviation
Type of employment	Waged work	54	77.1	7.8	11.1
	Non-waged work	16	22.9	11.4	13.6
Type of work hours	Full-time	35	64.8	4.2	5.8
	Part-time	19	35.2	14.5	15.1
Type of occupation	Specialist or manager	22	31.4	7.3	12.0
	Office worker	22	31.4	6.2	10.3
	Service worker	18	25.7	10.9	12.6
	Manufacturing worker	8	11.5	17.3	16.3
Earned income (won[a])	Under 500,000	9	12.9	4.1	3.1
	500,000–1,000,000	27	38.6	12.8	14.1
	500,000–1,500,000	22	31.4	6.3	10.1
	Over 1,500,000	12	17.1	6.8	10.9
Length of service (years)	Under 5 years	38	54.3	12.9	13.4
	Over 5 years	32	45.7	3.5	6.6

a: 1 US dollar = 930 Korean Won

As presented above, in terms of the characteristics of their job before childbirth, the career-interruption period was shortest in women who had been full-time office workers before childbirth, whose income was less than 500,000 won and whose length of service was more than five years.

Characteristics by return-to-work decisions and period of absence

Table 5.6 shows the characteristics of women who returned to the labour market after childbirth and of those who did not. With regard to demographic characteristics, those who were aged over thirty years represented 25.7 per cent of the women who returned to their job, and 8.6 per cent of those who did not. The average age of those who did return to their job was 27.8, which is 1.3 years older than 26.5, the average age of those who did not return.

The percentage of those who were college graduates or had higher academic qualifications was 31.4 per cent of the women who returned and 10.3 per cent of the women who did not return. The average length of education was 13.8 years in women who returned, which is 1.2 years longer than the 12.6 years in women who did not return. With regard to household characteristics, 38.6 per cent of women who returned to the labour market had a child-carer before returning to the labour market but only 10.3 per cent of women who did not return had one. In addition, the husband's average monthly income was 58,000 won more in women who did not return to their job than in those who did. As for the characteristics of occupation, the rate of return to the labour market was higher among women who had been non-waged workers before childbirth. With regard to the type of working hours, 64.8 per cent of full-time workers returned to the labour market, as opposed to 83.6 per cent of part-time workers. In relation to job category, 57.7 per cent of women who did not return to their job had been office workers before childbirth; while the average earned income at their job before childbirth was around 66,000 won higher and the average length of service around fifteen months longer in women who did return to their job.

These results show that college graduates' high academic qualifications affect their return to the labour market after childbirth, and that child-rearing is a critical factor in making decisions on labour supply after childbirth. Moreover, the fact that the husband's income was higher in women who did not return to the labour market after childbirth than in those who did supports the theory of labour supply in which women tend to avoid market labour when their husband's income level is high.

In addition, the fact that women who had been non-waged workers before childbirth show a high return-rate suggests that it is quite difficult for non-waged workers to return to the labour market after childbirth in the form of waged labour, which strongly reflects employers' decision-making. Moreover, if a woman had been a full-time worker and was paid a stable wage before childbirth, she would be highly likely to return to the labour market after childbirth. With this basic analysis alone, however, it is hard to conclude that these characteristics determine women's return to the labour market after childbirth. Factors affecting the transition from career-interruption after childbirth to re-entry into the labour market will be analysed systematically in the model analysis.

Table 5.7 compares the characteristics of women who returned to the labour market according to the duration from childbirth to their return, grouping them based on a two-month maternity-leave period.

Table 5.6: Characteristics according to whether returning to the labour market after childbirth

Characteristic	Variables	Whether returning to the labour market			
		Returned (n=70)		Not returned (n=58)	
		No. of cases	Percentage/average	No. of cases	Percentage/average
Demographic characteristics					
Age	Less than 30	52	74.3	53	91.4
	Over 30	18	25.7	5	8.6
	Average (years)		27.8		26.5
Academic qualification	High school and below	31	44.3	44	75.9
	Two-year college	17	24.3	8	13.8
	Four-year college and above	22	31.4	6	10.3
	Average (years)		13.8		12.6
Household characteristics					
Child-carer	Existing	27	38.6	6	10.3
	Not existing	43	61.4	52	89.7
Husband's income	Husband's average monthly income (won[a])		1,400,000		1,458,000
Occupational characteristics before childbirth					
Type of employment	Waged work	54	77.1	55	94.8
	Non-waged work	16	22.9	3	5.2
Type of work time	Full-time	35	64.8	9	16.4
	Part-time	19	35.2	46	83.6
Type of occupation	Specialist or manager	22	32.4	9	17.3
	Office worker	24	35.3	30	57.7
	Service worker	18	26.5	10	19.2
	Manufacturing worker	6	5.8	3	5.8
Earned income	Average monthly wage (won[a])	70	979,000	58	913,000
Length of service	Length of service (months)	70	56.0	58	41.4

a: US 1 dollar = 930 Korean Won

The legal length of maternity leave under the current law, which was revised in November 2001, is ninety days, but the data for this research was collected before the revision. The Korea Labor Panel conducts surveys from April to September every year and the law was revised in November 2001, meaning that even the data for this research corresponding to the year 2001 was collected before the revision. We thus applied the length of maternity leave as it was before the revision of the law, and grouped our respondents on the assumption that the length of maternity leave was sixty days.

As examined above, seventy out of the 128 respondents of this study returned to the labour market after childbirth. The period from childbirth to the return to the labour market was less than two months in forty-three women, and more than two months in twenty-seven of them. In terms of demographic characteristics, the average age was 2.4 years older in women who returned early—within two months from childbirth. In addition, women aged over thirty comprised 39.5 per cent of those who returned within two months but a mere 3.7 per cent of those who returned after two months or more, thus showing a difference in average age. As for academic qualifications among demographic characteristics, the percentage of those who were college graduates or had even higher academic qualifications was 39.6 per cent of women who returned within two months, much higher than the 18.5 per cent of women who returned after two months or more. In addition, 66.7 per cent of women who returned more than two months postpartum were only high-school graduates or had even lower academic qualifications.

In terms of household characteristics, the percentage of those who had a child-carer was 53.5 per cent among women who returned within two months but only 14.8 per cent among women who returned after two or more months. Furthermore, the husband's average monthly income was 1,425,000 won in women who returned within two months, which is 64,000 won higher than the 1,361,000 won in women who returned after two months or more.

With regard to the characteristics of occupation before childbirth, most of the women who returned within two months had been full-time specialists or managers and their average monthly income had been 1,154,000 won—208,000 won higher than the 946,000 won which was the average monthly income of women who returned after two or more months. Moreover, the average length of service was two times longer in women who returned within two months than in those who returned later than two months after childbirth. Summing up these results, it is concluded that those who return to the labour market early, within two months from childbirth, are more likely to have high academic qualifications and to be high-income professional managers, while those who return after two or more months are more likely to have low academic qualifications, relatively low income, and to be service workers.

Table 5.7: Characteristics according to duration until return

Characteristic	Value	Duration until return to the labour market			
		Within 2 months (n=43)		Beyond 2 months (n=27)	
		No. of cases	Percentage/ average	No. of cases	Percentage/ average
Demographic characteristics					
Age	Less than 30	26	60.5	26	96.3
	Over 30	17	39.5	1	3.7
	Average (years)		28.7		26.3
Academic qualification	High school and below	13	30.2	18	66.7
	Two-year college	13	30.2	4	14.8
	Four-year college and above	17	39.6	5	18.5
	Average (years)		14.3		12.9
Household characteristics					
Child-carer	Existing	23	53.5	4	14.8
	Not existing	20	46.5	23	85.2
Husband's income	Husband's average monthly income (won[a])		1,425,000		1,361,000
Occupational characteristics before childbirth					
Type of employment	Waged work	36	83.7	18	66.7
	Non-waged work	7	16.3	9	33.3
Type of work hours	Full-time	35	81.4	7	25.9
	Part-time	8	18.6	20	74.1
Type of occupation	Specialist or manager	17	39.5	5	18.5
	Office worker	16	37.2	8	29.6
	Service worker	6	14.0	12	44.4
	Manufacturing worker	4	2.3	2	7.5
Earned income	Average monthly wage (won[a])		1,154,000		946,000
Length of service	Length of service (months)		74.2		27.0
Duration until return	Duration from childbirth to return (months)		2		19.1

a: 1 dollar = 930 Korean Won

Factors determining return to the labour market after childbirth

Table 5.8 shows the result of Cox's proportional-hazards model, using as the dependent variable the hazard rate during the period from childbirth to re-entry to the labour market. According to the results of this analysis, women's return to the labour market after childbirth was affected by academic qualifications as a demographic characteristic, the presence or absence of a helper for child-rearing as a household characteristic, and job category and working hours as the characteristics of occupation before childbirth. First, among demographic variables, age appeared not to have an effect, as in Models 1 and 2. This is probably because the 128 respondents analysed in this study were mostly young, married women who had had their first child after 1997, and were similar in age.

With regard to academic qualifications, the rate of return to the labour market was 2.1 times higher in women who were two-year college graduates or had higher academic qualifications than in those who were high-school graduates or had lower academic qualifications. This supports the human capital theory, which says that participation in the labour market is higher among those with high academic qualifications. This result also reflects an improvement in young women's education levels. On the other hand, considering that women with high academic qualifications had been frustrated by a lack of jobs providing adequate rewards in the labour market in the past, the results suggest that job opportunities have been increasing in the labour market for young married women with high academic qualifications, and that the labour market has been restructured to accommodate that change.

As for the presence or absence of a child-carer among the characteristics of the household, the rate of return to the labour market was 2.1 times higher in women with a child-carer than in those without. This result emphasises that the existence of a child-carer is the biggest matter in determining whether a woman returns to the labour market after childbirth.

Only the type of employment and the type of working hours among the characteristics of occupation before childbirth appeared to have a significant effect on married women's return to the labour market after childbirth. This means that non-waged workers can return relatively easily to the labour market after childbirth in comparison to waged workers, but, on the other hand, it also means that married women are faced with a relatively high barrier to waged work and that the cost of maintaining a waged job is also high.

As for the type of working hours, the rate of return to the labour market was 3.4 times higher in women who had been full-time workers before childbirth than in those who had been part-time

Table 5.8: Factors determining married women's return to the labour market: Cox regression analysis

Variable	Value	Model 1	Model 2	Model 3
Demographic characteristics				
Age	Age	0.04 (1.04)	0.03 (1.04)	0.01 (1.01)
Academic qualifications	Two-year college and above (High school and below)	0.85 (2.30)^b	0.88 (2.40)^b	0.73 (2.08)^a
Household characteristics				
Husband's income	Natural log of husband's average monthly income		−0.21 (0.81)	−0.27 (0.77)
Child-carer	Existing (Not existing)		1.05 (2.86)^c	0.73 (2.08)^a
Occupational characteristics before childbirth				
Type of employment	Waged work (Non-waged work)			−1.46 (.23)^c
Type of work hours	Full-time (Part-time)			1.22 (3.38)^c
Type of occupation	Specialist or manager (Other)			0.05 (0.96)
Earned income	Natural log of average earned income			0.16 (1.17)
Length of service	Length of service at the workplace			0.001 (1.00)
−2log likelihood		623.43	608.50	586.16
χ^2		14.92	29.86	52.20
Increase of χ^2			14.94^c	22.34^c
Number of cases			128	
Number of events			70	
Number of censored cases (%)			58 (45.3)	

a= p<.05, b= p<.01, c= p<.001
( ): hazard rate

workers. Contrary to our expectation that the structural environment of a flexible labour market would allow married women to do work at home and workplace simultaneously, interruption in work-career was higher in part-time female workers than in full-time female workers.

Conclusions from empirical analysis

In this research, the effect of academic qualifications as human capital was clear on married women's return to the labour market after childbirth. This shows that young married women who have graduated from universities are participating in the labour market actively and that the condition of the labour market has improved. On the other hand, however, the results suggest that job opportunities in the labour market for women with children are difficult to access for those with low academic qualifications and, consequently, that women with low academic qualifications are at risk of falling into continuous, involuntary unemployment. Accordingly, it is necessary to recognise the polarised characteristics of labour supply by married women, to investigate groups of women in a relatively disadvantaged state, and to make policies to provide them with active support.

Secondly, we found that it takes a long time for married women to return to the labour market after birth. This shows that there is an urgent need to give return-to-work training to women who have long been unemployed involuntarily due to child-rearing. At present, vocational training and employment services for married women do not operate efficiently. One reason is that institutions commissioned by the government to conduct vocational training exclude married women who have been out of the labour market for a long time because, if the employment rate of the trainees is low, the government stops subsidies and, as a result, the institutions in question prefer young men whose possibility of employment is high. Thus, it is necessary to expand vocational training institutions specifically targeting married women.

Thirdly, this research shows that the rate of return to the labour market is twice as high among women who have a child-carer before returning to the labour market than those without a child-carer. It has been continuously emphasised in relevant policies and research that the resolution of the child-rearing burden is the starting-point for innovative improvement in the utilisation of the female labour force, and there has been a quest for solutions, centring on cases in more developed countries. Compared to more developed countries, though, Korea is in an early stage, and one of the fundamental reasons for the gap is the difference in the way of looking at childbirth. That is, more developed countries regard women's childbirth as production of a national human resource, and therefore make a huge investment in it, but in Korea childbirth is still regarded as the addition of a family member or a personal life event, so the government's investment and support for relevant policies is insufficient. If childbirth and child-rearing are understood in this latter way, it will be difficult to implement plans to resolve the burden of child-rearing, which demands continuous, long-term investment.

Fourthly, in this research, it was found that the transition rate from career interruption to return to the labour market is lower in women who had been waged workers before childbirth than in those who had been non-waged workers. This suggests that non-waged labour makes it easier for women to return to the labour market after childbirth, so it can be an alternative to preventing career interruption by childbirth. In addition, the fact that it is easier for non-waged workers than for their waged counterparts to return to the labour market after childbirth can be explained by the high flexibility and autonomy of non-waged labour, compared to waged labour. In general, after childbirth, women need more time for household labour. Thus, rather than waged labour with fixed working hours, non-waged labour in which the hours of household labour and market labour can be adjusted depending on the worker's situation eases career interruption after childbirth and enables a continuous labour supply. We therefore need to continue research on whether non-waged labour with flexible working hours can be a solution for preventing or easing women's career interruption, and to establish policies based on the results.

Limitations of empirical analysis

This study, which made microscopic analysis of married women's career interruption and their return to the labour market, centring on childbirth, which is the fundamental reason for the M-shaped economic activity participation rate in Korean women, has a number of limitations, as follows:

Firstly, we were faced with a problem in analysing and interpreting married women's childbirth separately from the complicatedly entangled chains of low utilisation and career interruption in the female labour force. Factors hindering women's economic activities include: education which implants gender-role prejudices in society, where distorted, fixed ideas on women are prevalent; a gender-discriminatory personnel management system and practices in the workplace; the lack of motherhood protection and insufficient childcare support after marriage and childbirth; and the inefficiency of institutions for re-employment training and employment stability. All these factors are linked to one another and form a large cycle. As the present study analysed only a part of the cycle separately, it might distort the overall context of factors hindering women's economic activities. For this reason, our study was highly limited in terms of in-depth examination. Subsequent research needs to make in-depth analysis of each stage and interpret the results within the whole context.

Secondly, there were problems related to the limitations of our data. In conducting systematic model analysis reflecting all the demographic characteristics, household characteristics and the characteristics of jobs before childbirth using four years' worth of panel data, this study limited its samples for model analysis to women who had experienced childbirth since 1997, rather than all married women included in the data. Here, we note that the number of samples was so small that it may have lowered the reliability of the results of our analysis.

In addition, this study limited its respondents for model analysis to young married women, so it could not examine trends in the whole group of married women or differences among age groups. Moreover, in model analysis we used the Cox hazards regression model, one of the dynamic analysis methods, in order to overcome the limitations of static analysis, but could not maximise the advantages of dynamic analysis because the follow-up period of the panel was short and the estimated value was likely to be similar to the value of the regression coefficient in logistic regression analysis, due to the small number of events of return to the labour market after childbirth. These data limitations became obstacles to in-depth systematic model analysis.

Thirdly, there were problems in the present researcher's arbitrary assumptions in analysis. For example, in the case of women who returned to the labour market within two months, we could not distinguish whether the return was due to the women's own decision or by a requirement of her workplace at the end of her maternity leave, so the present researcher divided the cases on the basis of the legal number of days for maternity leave. What is more, in the model analysis of labour-market return, a woman was regarded as employed before childbirth if she had been working at least ten months before the date of childbirth. The period for reflecting women's employment state before childbirth was set somewhat long in order to avoid the omission of cases of those who had quit their job due to pregnancy, but this assumption had the limitation of expanding a small number of cases.

Implications of Korean cases to female labour policy in Japan

Korea and Japan have very similar structures in their pattern of women's lifelong participation in economic activities. As is the case with the rate of Korean women's participation in economic activities by age, that of their Japanese counterparts also shows an M-shaped structure, which has two peaks at the ages of the late twenties and early thirties, with the lowest point at the ages of thirty to thirty-four. Though the degree of Japanese women's participation in economic activities at the ages of thirty to thirty-four (60.3 per cent), at which they show the lowest rate of economic participation due to childbirth and childcare, appears relatively higher than that of Korean women's economic participation at the same age (49.3 per cent) (ILO 2004), Japan is no different from Korea in terms of the interruption of married women's employment due to childbirth and childcare. The reason for the somewhat flatter M-shaped curve of Japanese women's labour is late marriage and late childbirth—that is to say, the shallowing of the dip in the Japanese M-curve has resulted not from the continuation of Japanese women's employment regardless of marriage, childbirth and childcare, but from an increase in the employment rate of single women and married women without children (Japanese Cabinet Office 2006). We can more clearly explicate this point if we investigate the labour trend in women aged twenty-five to twenty-nine years. By comparing the Japanese Ministry of Internal Affairs and Communications' 1987 Employment Status Survey with its 2004 counterpart, we can see that the proportion of unmarried women in the labour market has increased from 37.6 per cent in 1987 to 58.4 per cent in 2004, whereas the rate of working married women with their last child under the age of three has dropped from 33.1 per cent in 1987 to 20.6 per cent in 2004.

Though the number of Japanese women who hope to continue their work along with childcare after childbirth is rapidly increasing, in reality the common trend is for them to be re-employed after ceasing their jobs rather than to maintain the compatibility of work and home (Japanese Cabinet Office 2006). This means that Japan does not have an environment in which women can maintain the compatibility of work and childcare. As is explicated from the results of the empirical analysis of Korean data, if there is another carer, the likelihood of a woman returning to the labour market is twice as high, or more. Though the Japanese government has tried to increase the accommodation capacity of childcare institutions by implementing its so-called 'Angel Plan' and 'New Angel Plan' initiatives, there are still many children on waiting lists in big cities, and thus the rates of female employment in those areas with a high number of children awaiting admittance to childcare facilities are known to be low. In addition to this, it has been reported that due to the limitations of such services as extended childcare, night-time childcare and holiday childcare, women need to shoulder a great burden (Japanese Cabinet Office 2006).

Above all, in addition to recognition of a gender-role distinction which insists that women should take full charge of childcare, because Japanese workers experience long working hours, the fact that husbands are not willing to participate in childcare is one of the main reasons for the increased burden of bringing up children being placed upon women and governments. This suggests that a change in Japanese society's basic recognition of childcare is the most urgent matter. That is to say, men are not exempt from the problem of the compatibility of work and home, and thus the necessary changes in the recognition of childcare and concrete efforts to encourage men's participation in childcare should be carried out constantly in Japanese society, along with improvement in services such as childcare institutions and various other childcare facilities.

As is often the case, a woman who is re-employed after going through a difficult period of childcare usually returns to part-time labour with low wages and monotonous work. This is because a decline in her work ability follows, due to her long spell of career-interruption. As a result, it becomes difficult for her to be employed as a regular worker. Though the decline in job-skills cannot be simply evaluated, it can be indirectly grasped through wage-comparison. According to the Japanese Ministry of Internal Affairs and Communications' 2004 Labour Force Survey, the longer the period of a woman's career interruption, the lower her wages will be at any position she acquires after re-employment, compared to her previous position. If those married women who have experienced career-interruption due to childbirth and childcare are assigned only to low-waged, monotonous work in the labour market, there will be an expansion in female temporary and irregular workers. This means that Japanese society does not affirmatively utilise its female labour force, and that it is, in the end, passive in securing highly-skilled female workers.

Considering the results of the empirical analysis of Korean cases—that women with high educational experience are more likely to return to the labour market after career interruption—it seems necessary for Japanese society to initiate a plan to prevent the loss of excellent female resources who have the intention to be re-employed after a temporary lapse in job skills, and to attract them positively to the labour market. Needless to say, it is very necessary to prevent such a decline of job skills in order to create a labour-market environment which allows the compatibility of work and home, so that married women wanting constant employment can continue their career without ceasing their work. However, those women who want to be re-employed after some period of job interruption need a system that can obviate any decline in job skills during the period of job interruption. In addition to a system which provides constant off-the-job-training, another plan is needed that can lead those female resources remaining unemployed to be re-employed, by introducing a system which provides steps by which they can be regular employees through on-the-job training after returning to a temporary job. This will be an alternative which can secure female resources by cultivating and utilising them as high-quality human resources beyond the re-employment structure in which only married women rotate among low-waged, monotonous jobs such as those in sales and service industries. It can also be an alternative way to attract highly-educated women who are passive in relation to job-seeking activities to the labour market. On the other hand, it should be noted that the most necessary task is to facilitate an employment environment and labour market conditions in which a woman can have a good chance of employment and a decent job when she tries to be re-employed after childcare, so that having to maintain continuous employment will not be the only way for a woman to remain in an advantageous position in Japanese society.

Notes

Chapter 2

1 In Japan, if wives reside with their husband's parents, those wives tend to work outside the home to avoid intergenerational conflict. Women's employment rate in three-generational households is therefore generally high.
2 The present author was permitted to use NFRJ03 through the endorsement of the National Family Research Committee of the Japan Society of Family Sociology. Also, the author used NFRJ98 by way of the Social Science Japan Data Archive at the University of Tokyo.
3 A Type II error is an error in statistical estimation when a null hypothesis was not rejected. It happens when the null hypothesis is not supported in the population, but the estimation from the data could not reject that null hypothesis. Though its probability usually cannot be calculated, it is well known that Type II error increases as the sample size decreases. The only way to diminish Type II error is to use large-sample-size data.

Chapter 4

1 Some researchers (e.g. Bielby and Bielby 1984; Hakim 1991; Hakim 1996: 84–86) on married women's employment argue that, in theory, married women's intention or commitment is more relevant to women's decision on employment than gender ideology or gender-role attitudes in general. I emphasise, however, that even gender ideology is strongly associated with women's employment, as I will show in the following discussion.
2 The simultaneous existence of the three negative associations between the three variables is not a genuine paradox in a logical or statistical sense. Nevertheless, this may *seem* paradoxical because, in ordinary situations, we feel that transitivity holds not only for a 'logically strict' implication, that is, 'If A, then (always) B,' but also for a 'weak' implication, that is, 'If A, then (generally,

frequently, often, et cetera) B,' though transitivity really does not hold for a 'weak' implication (cf. Boudon 1971: 10–24).

3 Some readers may see in Figure 4.2 a 'polarisation' among those who attained a higher education because the percentage of full-time workers ('Employer/Full-time employee') who gained a higher education is also greater than that of full-time workers who did not attain a higher education. Looking closely at the occupations of the full-time workers, however, I found the following difference between those who had attained a higher education and those who had not: on the one hand, most full-time workers with a higher education have professional occupations—many of which require the credentials of a university- or junior-college graduate—and/or are employed in the public sector; on the other hand, though, most full-time workers without a higher education are clerical or sales workers in the private sector. In Japan, professional workers, such as school teachers, and employees in the public sector find more advantage in continuing their work-career than do clerical or sales workers in the private sector. Using data from the fourth and fifth surveys on 'Social Stratification and Social Mobility' in Japan (SSM85 and SSM95 Surveys), Tanaka (1997) shows that, if we exclude school teachers, Japanese married women's education has no significant effect on their continuity rate in full-time employment even if we take into account their husband's occupational status and their own occupational status before marriage.

4 Another theory which would explain the associations between women's education, employment and gender-role attitudes is Hakim's (2000) 'preference theory.' (For example, see Table 3.4 in Hakim (2000: 78) and her interpretation of it.) Although Hakim (2000: chap. 2) blames current theorising on women's labour-market participation in the sociology of work and employment, labour economics and social psychology for their *post hoc* explanations, it seems to me that her theory cannot avoid a *post hoc* explanation or tautology, either.

5 In fact, crude analysis of data from the SSM95 Survey reveals that there exists not only a strong tendency of homogamy with respect to educational attainment, but also a higher correlation between the educational level and the income of husbands in Japan (See Appendix 4B). By themselves, however, these results do not imply that Japanese female high-school students who would like to enter universities or junior-colleges are motivated

to find prospective husbands who would earn higher amounts of money.

6 Lee (2001) also emphasises South Korean and Japanese women's motivation in terms of the value of higher education in the marriage market rather than in the labour market, though her data analysis is confined to male and female university graduates in South Korea.

7 This hypothesis is inspired by many previous studies on the coupling of the idea of rational choice and that of cognitive dissonance reduction (e.g. Akerlof 1989; Akerlof and Dickens 1982; Dickens 1986; Elster 1983; Montgomery 1994; Opp 1989: chap. 8; Rabin 1994).

8 In Japan, though the Equal Employment Opportunity Law has since 1985 prohibited a marriage bar, that is, the exclusion of married women from employment, no explicit penalties are imposed on employers who fail to observe the prohibition. For comparison in this respect between Japan, on the one hand, and European countries and the United States, on the other, see, for example, Brinton (1993: 229–234), Cohen (1985: 97–115), Goldin (1990: 161–179), and Hakim (1996: 123–125).

9 If we assume 'imperfect information,' it is easy to explain the fact that though women who have rationally decided their life-course after schooling seldom attain the employment status that they have desired, some women nevertheless do invest time and money in higher education. However, even if we assume 'perfect information,' we can still explain this fact. For example, let us consider the situation supposed in Boudon's (1979: chap. 5) model of 'relative deprivation' (cf. Crosby 1976; Crosby 1982; Merton 1968: chap. 10; Runciman 1966; Stouffer, Suchman, DeVinney, Star and Williams 1949: 125; Walker and Smith 2002). In this situation, individuals compete for a scarce resource such as a higher status with higher rewards. There is a limitation on the number of individuals who can obtain the resource. The probability that one can get the resource depends on the number (or the proportion in the group) of individuals who bet on that resource. If, with perfect information, each individual chooses whether to bet on the grounds of the expected utility, the number of those who bet will exceed the number of individuals who can obtain the resource under a certain condition. (See note 11 for further examination of the relationship between cognitive dissonance and relative deprivation.)

10 I expect that female university- or junior-college graduates, that is, women who have attained a higher education, will be more likely to experience cognitive dissonance and change their gender ideology in reducing cognitive dissonance than women who have had only a secondary education at junior- or senior high-schools. This is because resistance to reduction of cognitive dissonance through changing employment status seems stronger for female university- or junior-college graduates who fail to continue their work-career after marriage or child-bearing than for women who attained only a secondary education and wanted to be homemakers after marriage, but who became part-time workers after marrying or giving birth. In the Japanese segmented labour market, it is difficult for female university- or junior-college graduates to re-enter the labour market as full-time workers after marriage or childbirth, while it is relatively easy for married women with only a secondary education who work part-time to quit their jobs or exit the labour market (and also to re-enter the labour market as part-time workers).

11 I anticipate an objection to this. Do women who have to abandon the work-career which they had hoped to pursue really feel psychological pressure to reduce their cognitive dissonance? Why do they not feel relative deprivation and dissatisfaction, instead? In reply to such an objection, I refer to a classical experiment on the relationship between cognitive dissonance and relative deprivation and a recent re-formulation of cognitive dissonance. On the one hand, Brehm and Cohen (1959) found, by their experiments, the following tendency: under the condition that the participants have to commit to a situation which involves distribution of rewards, the higher the degree of relative deprivation, the greater will be the participants' dissatisfaction with the result of the distribution of rewards; under the condition that the participants can choose whether to commit to such a situation, the greater the degree of relative deprivation, the more satisfied will the participants be with the result of the reward-distribution. On the other hand, by focusing on the function of self-concept, Thibodeau and Aronson (1992) tried to explain why some experiments on the relationship between cognitive dissonance and attitude-change support predictions from Festinger's (1957) original theory of cognitive dissonance, while other experiments do not. They argued that the psychological pressure for a person to reduce cognitive dissonance arises only

in situations which involve an effort to maintain his or her self-concept as someone who is competent and morally good. Now, my hypothesis postulates that women are rational and competent subjects who can decide their own life-course after schooling. If they have to abandon the course that they have decided, their self-concept as a competent person will be threatened. I thus predict that women who have to abandon the work-career they had hoped to pursue tend to experience attitude-change through cognitive dissonance reduction, rather than to experience dissatisfaction or frustration caused by relative deprivation.

12 We also find a very weak association not only between female high-school students' gender ideology and that of their mothers, but also between that of the same students and their fathers. The proportion of those who approve of the gendered division of labour is nineteen per cent among female high-school students whose mothers approve of the gendered division of labour, while the proportion of those who approve of the gendered division of labour is eighteen per cent among female high-school students whose mothers disapprove of the gendered division of labour ($r = 0.017$). The proportion of those who approve of the gendered division of labour is twenty-two per cent among female high-school students whose fathers approve of the gendered division of labour, while the proportion of those who approve of the gendered division of labour is thirteen per cent among female high-school students whose fathers disapprove of the gendered division of labour ($r = 0.112$). These results provide evidence against Brinton's (1993) argument which assumes socialisation of daughters by parents as an important factor, although we cannot deny the possibility of spurious non-correlations.

References

Agresti, Alan (1996), *An Introduction to Categorical Data Analysis*, New York: John Wiley and Sons.
────── (2002) (1990), *Categorical Data Analysis*, 2nd ed., New York: John Wiley and Sons.
Akerlof, George A. (1989), 'The economics of illusion,' *Economics and Politics*, 1(1), pp. 1–15.
Akerlof, George A., and William T. Dickens (1982), 'The economic consequences of cognitive dissonance,' *American Economic Review*, 72(3), pp. 307–319.
Ammeter, Anthony P., Ceasar Douglas, William L. Gardner, Wayne A. Hochwarter and Gerald R. Ferris (2002), 'Toward a political theory of leadership,' *Leadership Quarterly*, 13, pp. 751–796.
Arai, Kazuhiro (1998) (1995), *The Economics of Education: An Analysis of College-Going Behavior*, Tokyo: Springer.
Asahi Shimbun (Asahi Newspaper) (2004), 'Asahi Shimbun zenkoku yoron chōsa: josei no shakai shinshutsu kōtei hachiwari (Asahi Shimbun national opinion poll: eighty per cent affirm women's social emergence), *Asahi Shimbun*, 20 November.
Bakan, David (1966), *The Duality of Human Existence: An Essay on Psychology and Religion*, Chicago: Rand McNally.
Barrow, Lisa (1999), 'An analysis of women's return-to-work decisions following first birth,' *Economic Inquiry*, 37(3), pp. 432–451.
Becker, Gary S. (1965), 'A theory of allocation of time,' *The Economic Journal*, 75, pp. 493–517.
────── (1993) (1964), *Human Capital: A Theoretical and Empirical Analysis with Special Reference to Education*, 3rd ed., Chicago: University of Chicago Press.
Becker, Jeffrey, Roya Ayman and Karen Korabik (2002), 'Discrepancies in self/subordinates' perceptions of leadership behaviour: leader's gender, organisational context, and leader's self-monitoring,' *Group and Organization Management*, 27, pp. 226–244.
Belsky, Jay, and John Kelly (1994), *The Transition to Parenthood*, New York: Delacorte Press.
Bem, Sandra L. (1974), 'The measurement of psychological androgyny,' *Journal of Consulting and Clinical Psychology*, 42, pp. 155–162.
Berdahl, Jennifer L. (1996), 'Gender and leadership in work groups: six alternative models,' *Leadership Quarterly*, 7, pp. 21–40.
Berger, Joseph, M. Hamit Fisek, Robert Z. Norman and Morris Zelditch Jr (1977), *Status Characteristics and Social Interaction: An Expectation-states Approach*, New York: Elsevier.
Berger, Joseph, David G. Wagner and Morris Zelditch Jr (1985), 'Introduction: Expectation states theory: review and assessment,' in Morris Zelditch Jr (ed.),

Theoretical Research Programs: Studies in the Growth of Theory, Stanford, California: Stanford University Press, pp. 1–72.

Bielby, Denise Del Vento, and William T. Bielby (1984), 'Work commitment, sex-role attitudes, and women's employment,' *American Sociological Review*, 49(2), pp. 234–247.

Bielby, William T., and James N. Baron (1986), 'Men and women at work: sex segregation and statistical discrimination,' *American Journal of Sociology*, 91(4), pp. 759–799.

Blake, R.R., and J.S. Mouton (1964), *The Managerial Grid*, Houston: Gulf.

Blau, David M., and Philip K. Robins (1988), 'Child-care costs and family labor supply,' *Review of Economics and Statistics*, 70, pp. 374–381.

Boudon, Raymond (1971), *Les Mathématiques en Sociologie*, Paris: Presses Universitaires de France.

―――― (1982) (1979), *The Unintended Consequences of Social Action*, London: Macmillan.

Brehm, Jack W., and Arthur R. Cohen (1959), 'Choice and chance relative deprivation as determinants of cognitive dissonance,' *Journal of Abnormal and Social Psychology*, 58(3), pp. 383–387.

Brinton, Mary C. (1993), *Women and the Economic Miracle: Gender and Work in Postwar Japan*, Berkeley: University of California Press.

―――― (ed.) (2001), *Women's Working Lives in East Asia*, Stanford, California: Stanford University Press.

Brinton, Mary C., Yean-Ju Lee and William L. Parish (1995), 'Married women's employment in rapidly industrializing societies: examples from East Asia,' *American Journal of Sociology*, 100(5), pp. 1099–1130.

Carbonell, Joyce L. (1984), 'Sex roles and leadership revisited,' *Journal of Applied Psychology*, 69, pp. 44–49.

Carli, Linda L. (2001), 'Gender and social influence,' *Journal of Social Issues*, 57, pp. 725–741.

Chang, Jiyeun (1997), 'Labor Force Withdrawal and Entry Surrounding First Childbirth of Married Women,' unpublished Ph.D. dissertation, University of Wisconsin-Madison.

Chang, Jiyeun, and Jikyung Kim (2001), 'Effects of childcare type and expenditure on married women's job discontinuation,' *Proceedings of the Third Annual Meeting of Korea Labor and Income Panel Study*, pp. 365–388.

Choe, Minja Kim, Larry L. Bumpass and Noriko O. Tsuya (2004), 'Employment,' in Noriko O. Tsuya and Larry L. Bumpass (eds), *Marriage, Work, and Family Life in Comparative Perspective: Japan, South Korea, and the United States*, Honolulu: University of Hawai'i Press, pp. 95–113.

Clifford, William B., and Patricia L. Tobin (1977), 'Labor force participation of working mothers and family formation: some further evidence,' *Demography*, 14(3), pp. 273–284.

Cohen, Samuel (1985), *The Process of Occupational Sex-Typing: The Feminization of Clerical Labor in Great Britain*, Philadelphia: Temple University Press.

Connelly, Rachel (1992), 'The effect of child care costs on married women's labor force participation,' *Review of Economics and Statistics*, 74, pp. 83–90.

Crosby, Faye J. (1976), 'A model of egoistical relative deprivation,' *Psychological Review*, 83(2), pp. 85–113.
——— (1982), *Relative Deprivation and Working Women*, New York: Oxford University Press.
Davies, Paul G., Steven J. Spencer and Claude M. Steele (2005), 'Clearing the air: identity safety moderates the effects of stereotype threat on women's leadership aspirations,' *Journal of Personality and Social Psychology*, 88, pp. 276–287.
Desai, Sonalde, and Linda J. Waite (1991), 'Women's employment during pregnancy and after the first birth: occupational characteristics and work commitment,' *American Sociological Review*, 56, pp. 551–566.
Dex, Shirley, Heather Joshi, Susan Macran and Andrew McCulloch (1998), 'Women's employment transitions around child bearing,' *Oxford Bulletin of Economics and Statistics*, 60(1), pp. 79–98.
Dickens, William T. (1986), 'Crime and punishment again: the economic approach with a psychological twist,' *Journal of Public Economics*, 30, pp. 97–107.
Dobbins, Gregory H., William S. Long, Esther J. Dedrick and Tayna C. Clemons (1990), 'The role of self-monitoring and gender on leader emergence: a laboratory and field study,' *Journal of Management*, 16, pp. 609–618.
Douglas, Paul Howard (1964) (1934, 1957), *The Theory of Wages*, 2nd ed., New York: A.M. Kelley.
Eagly, Alice H. (1987), *Sex Differences in Social Behavior: A Social-role Interpretation*, Hillsdale, New Jersey: Erlbaum.
Eagly, Alice H., Mary C. Johannesen-Schmidt and Marloes L. van-Engen (2003), 'Transformational, transactional and laissez-faire leadership styles: a meta-analysis comparing women and men,' *Psychological Bulletin*, 129, pp. 569–591.
Eagly, Alice H., and Blair T. Johnson (1990), 'Gender and leadership style: a meta-analysis,' *Psychological Bulletin*, 108, pp. 233–256.
Eagly, Alice H., and Steven J. Karau (2002), 'Role congruity theory of prejudice toward female leaders,' *Psychological Review*, 109, pp. 573–598.
Eagly, Alice H., Steven J. Karau and Mona G. Makhijani (1995), 'Gender and the effectiveness of leaders: a meta-analysis,' *Psychological Bulletin*, 117, pp. 125–145.
Eagly, Alice H., Mona G. Makhijani and Bruce G. Klonsky (1992), 'Gender and the evaluation of leaders: a meta-analysis,' *Psychological Bulletin*, 111, pp. 3–22.
Eby, Lillian T., Jailza Cader and Carrie L. Noble (2003), 'Why do high self-monitors emerge as leaders in small groups? A comparative analysis of the behaviors of high versus low self-monitors,' *Journal of Applied Social Psychology*, 33, pp. 1457–1479.
Elster, Jon (1983), *Sour Grapes: Studies in the Subversion of Rationality*, Cambridge: Cambridge University Press.
Eurostat (2005), *Europe in Figures: Eurostat Yearbook 2005*, Brussels, Belgium: Eurostat Publications.
Eurostat, European Commission (2004), *How Europeans Spend Their Time: Everyday Life of Women and Men* (2004 ed.), Luxembourg: European Communities.

Even, William E. (1987), 'Career interruptions following childbirth,' *Journal of Labor Economics*, 5(2), pp. 255–277.
Fagenson, Ellen A. (1990), 'Perceived masculine and feminine attributes examined as a function of individuals' sex and level in the organisational power hierarchy: a test of four theoretical perspectives,' *Journal of Applied Psychology*, 75, pp. 204–211.
Felmlee, Diane H. (1984), 'A dynamic analysis of women's employment exit,' *Demography*, 21, pp. 171–183.
Festinger, Leon (1957), *A Theory of Cognitive Dissonance*, Stanford, California: Stanford University Press.
Fiedler, Fred E. (1967), *A Theory of Leadership Effectiveness*, New York: McGraw-Hill.
Foels, Rob, James E. Driskell, Brian Mullen and Eduardo Salas (2000), 'The effects of democratic leadership on group member satisfaction: an integration,' *Small Group Research*, 31, pp. 676–701.
Fuwa, Makiko (2004), 'Gender and housework in 22 countries,' *American Sociological Review*, 69, pp. 751–767.
Fuwa, Makiko, and Jun'ya Tsutsui (2006), 'Kaji buntan ni taisuru fukōheikan no kokusai hikaku bunseki (International comparative analysis of fairness feeling about sharing household work),' paper presented at the 16th annual meeting of Japan Society of Family Sociology.
Gardiner, Maria, and Marika Tiggemann (1999), 'Gender differences in leadership style, job stress and mental health in male- and female-dominated industries,' *Journal of Occupational and Organizational Psychology*, 72, pp. 301–315.
Garrett, Patricia, Deeann Wenk and Sally Lubeck (1990), 'Working around childbirth: comparative and empirical perspectives on parental-leave policy,' *Child Welfare*, 69(5), pp. 401–413.
Gastil, John (1994), 'A meta-analytic review of the productivity and satisfaction of democratic and autocratic leadership,' *Small Group Research*, 25, pp. 384–410.
Goktepe, Janet R., and Craig Eric Schneier (1989), 'Role of sex, gender roles, and attraction in predicting emergent leaders,' *Journal of Applied Psychology*, 74, pp. 165–167.
Goldin, Claudia (1990), *Understanding the Gender Gap: An Economic History of American Women*, New York: Oxford University Press.
Graen, George B., and Mary Uhl-Bien (1995), 'Relationship-based approach to leadership: development of leader-member exchange (LMX) theory of leadership over 25 years: applying a multi-level multi-domain perspective,' *Leadership Quarterly*, 6, pp. 219–247.
Greenstein, Theodore (1989), 'Human capital, marital and birth timing, and the postnatal labor force participation of married women,' *Journal of Family Issues*, 10(3), pp. 359–382.
——— (1996), 'Gender ideology and perceptions of the fairness of the division of household labor: effects on marital quality,' *Social Forces*, 74, pp. 1029–1042.
Hakim, Catherine (1991), 'Grateful slaves and self-made women: fact and fantasy in women's work orientation,' *European Sociological Review*, 7(2), pp. 101–121.

―――― (1996), *Key Issues in Women's Work: Female Heterogeneity and the Polarisation of Women's Employment*, London: Athlone Press.

―――― (2000), *Work–Lifestyle Choices in the 21st Century: Preference Theory*, Oxford: Oxford University Press.

Hall, Rosalie J., Judd W. Workman and Christopher A. Marchioro (1998), 'Sex, task, and behavioral flexibility effects on leadership perceptions,' *Organizational Behavior and Human Decision Processes*, 74, pp. 1–32.

Halpin, Andrew W., and Ben J. Winer (1957), 'A factorial study of the leader behaviour description,' in R.M. Stogdill and A.E. Coons (eds), *Leader Behavior: Its Description and Measurement*, Columbus, Ohio: Bureau of Business Research, Ohio State University.

Hara, Junsuke, and Yoshiko Hiwano (1990), 'Seibetsu yakuwari ishiki to shufu no chii hyōka (Japanese women's gender role attitudes and evaluation of the status of homemakers),' in Hideo Okamoto and Michiko Naoi (eds), *Josei to shakai kaisō* (Women and social stratification), *Gendai Nihon no kaisō kōzō* (The structure of social stratification in contemporary Japan), vol. 4, Tokyo: University of Tokyo Press, pp. 165–186.

Hara, Junsuke, and Kazuo Seiyama (2005), *Inequality amid Affluence: Social Stratification in Japan* (Stratification and Inequality Series, The Center for the Study of Social Stratification and Inequality, Tohoku University, vol. 1.), translated by Brad Williams, Melbourne: Trans Pacific Press.

Harmon-Jones, Eddie, and Judson Mills (eds) (1999), *Cognitive Dissonance: Progress on a Pivotal Theory in Social Psychology*, Washington, DC: American Psychological Association.

Hashimoto, Kenji (1999), *Gendai Nihon no kaikyū kōzō* (Class structure in contemporary Japan), Tokyo: Tōshindō.

Heckman, James (1974), 'Effects of child-care programs on women's work effort,' *Journal of Political Economy*, 82(2), pp. s136–s163.

Hochschild, Arlie (1989), *The Second Shift: Working Parents and the Revolution at Home*, New York: Viking Press.

Hollander, Edwin P., and Janice D. Yoder (1980), 'Some issues in comparing women and men as leaders,' *Basic and Applied Social Psychology*, 1, pp. 267–280.

Hooijberg, Robert (1996), 'A multidirectional approach toward leadership: an extension of the concept of behavioural complexity,' *Human Relations*, 49, pp. 917–946.

Horne-Kawashima, Yoko (1985), *Joshi rōdō to rōdō shijō kōzō no bunseki* (Analyses of women's work and the structure of the labor market.), Tokyo: Nihon Keizai Hyōron-sha.

House, Robert J., and Gary Dessler (1974), 'The path-goal theory of leadership: some post hoc and a priori tests,' in J.G. Hunt and L.L. Larson (eds), *Contingency Approaches to Leadership: A Symposium Held at Southern Illinois University, Carbondale, May 17–18, 1973*, Carbondale, Illinois: Southern Illinois University Press, pp. 29–55.

Inaba, Akihide (1999a), 'Kazoku seikatsu, shokugyō seikatsu, ikuji: ikuji to yakuwari sutorein no kōzō (Family life, work life, and child-rearing: structure of child-care and role strain),' in Kunio Ishihara (ed.), *Tsumatachi no seikatsu sutoresu to sapōto kankei: kazoku, shokugyō, nettowāku*

(Women's life stress and supportive relationships: family, occupation, and networks), Tokyo: Tokyo Metropolitan University Press, pp. 29–51.
────── (1999b), 'Naze jōko josei no sutorein ga takaku nai no ka? (Why are fully-employed women's role strains not so high?),' in Kunio Ishihara (ed.), *Tsuma-tachi no seikatsu sutoresu to sapōto kankei: kazoku, shokugyō, nettowāku* (Women's life stress and supportive relationships: family, occupation, and networks), Tokyo: Tokyo Metropolitan University Press, pp. 53–85.
────── (2005), 'Kazoku to shōshi-ka (The family and below-replacement fertility in Japan),' *Shakaigaku Hyōron (Japanese Sociological Review),* 56(1), pp. 38–54.
International Labour Organization (2004), *Yearbook of Labour Statistics.*
Iwasawa, Miho (2003), 'Tsuma no shūgyō to shusshō-ryoku (Wife's employment and fertility),' in Kokuritsu Shakai Hoshō Kenkyūjo (ed.), *Waga kuni fūfu no kekkon katei to shusshō-ryoku: dai 12-kai shusshō dōkō kihon chōsa* (Marriage of Japanese couples and fertility: twelfth basic survey on fertility trends), Tokyo: Kōsei Tōkei Kyōkai (Health and Welfare Statistics Association), pp. 66–88.
Japanese Cabinet Office (2006), *White Paper on the National Lifestyle.*
Johnes, Geraint (1999), 'Schooling, fertility and the labour market experience of married women,' *Applied Econometrics,* 31, pp. 585–592.
Jones, Edward E., and Richard E. Nisbett (1971), 'The actor and the observer: divergent perceptions of the causes of behaviour,' in Edward E. Jones, David E. Kanouse, Harold H. Kelley, Richard E. Nisbett, Stuart Valins and Bernard Weiner (eds), *Attribution: Perceiving the causes of behaviour,* Morristown, New Jersey: General Learning Press, pp. 79–94.
Kanai, Toshihiro (2003), *Kyaria dezain gaido: jibun no kyaria o umaku furikaeri tenbō suru* (Career design guide: Effectively reflecting upon and developing your own career), Tokyo: Hakutō Shobō.
Kashiwagi, Keiko (2006), 'Kazoku/oyako kankei to jendā (Family/parent–child relationships and gender), in Atsuko Suzuki and Keiko Kashiwagi, *Jendā no shinrigaku* (Psychology of gender: New perspectives on mind and behaviour. World of psychology specialist editions, 5), Tokyo: Baifūkan, pp. 127–146.
Kawakami, Christine, Judith B. White and Ellen J. Langer (2000), 'Mindful and masculine: freeing women leaders from the constraints of gender roles,' *Journal of Social Issues,* 56, pp. 49–63.
Kawashima, Yoko, and Toshiaki Tachibanaki (1986), 'The effect of discrimination and of industry segmentation on Japanese wage differentials in relation to education,' *International Journal of Industrial Organization,* 4, pp. 43–68.
Kent, Russell L., and Sherry E. Moss (1994), 'Effects of sex and gender role on leader emergence,' *Academy of Management Journal,* 37, pp. 1335–1346.
Kim, Youngok (1998), *Analysis of Dynamic Change in the Women's Labor Force,* Seoul: Korean Women's Development Institute.
Kimura, Kunihiro (1998), 'Kikon josei no gakureki, shūgyō-keitai to seibetsu yakuwari ishiki (Education, employment and gender ideology of Japanese married women),' in Fumiaki Ojima (ed.), *Jendā to kaisō ishiki* (Social and psychological functioning of gender and stratification), 1995 SSM (Social Stratification and Mobility) Survey Series, vol. 14, Tokyo:

Research Group for 1995 SSM (Social Stratification and Mobility) Survey, pp. 23–48.

―――― (2000), 'Rōdō shijō no kōzō to yūhaigū josei no ishiki (Structure of the labour market and social consciousness of married women in Japan),' in Kazuo Seiyama (ed.), *Jendā, shijō, kazoku* (Gender, market, and family), *Nihon no kaisō shisutemu* (Stratification system in Japan), vol. 4, Tokyo: The University of Tokyo Press, pp. 177–192.

―――― (2005), '"Josei ni totte no gakureki no imi" saikō: kyōiku, shūgyō to seibetsu yakuwari ishiki no kanren no jikeiretsu-teki hikaku (Reconsidering "the significance of education for Japanese women": a time-series analysis of education, occupation and gender role attitudes),' in Kazuo Katase, Kunihiro Kimura and Koji Abe (eds), *'Kyōiku to shakai ni taisuru kōkōsei no ishiki,' dai 5-ji chōsa hōkokusho* (Report on the fifth survey on 'Social consciousness of high school students and their parents'), Sendai: Research Group on Education and Culture, Tohoku University, pp. 57–70.

Klerman, Jacob Alex, and Arleen Leibowitz (1990), 'Child care and women's return to work after childbirth,' *American Economics Review*, 80(2), pp. 284–290.

―――― (1994), 'The work–employment distinction among new mothers,' *Journal of Human Resources*, 29(2), pp. 277–303.

Kokuren Kaihatsu Keikaku (United Nations Development Programme) (2006), *Ningen kaihatsu hōkokusho 2005* (Human development report 2005), Tokyo: Kokusai Kyōryoku Shuppan-kai (Japan International Cooperation Publishing Co., Ltd).

Kokuritsu Josei Kyōiku Kaikan (National Women's Education Centre) (2006), *Katei kyōiku ni kansuru kokusai hikaku chōsa* (International comparative survey on home education).

Kokuritsu Shakai Hoshō/Jinkō Mondai Kenkyūjo (National Institute of Population and Social Security Research) (2002), *Kekkon to shussan ni kansuru zenkoku chōsa (dokushin chōsa): dai-jūni-kai shussei dōkō kihon chōsa* (Nationwide survey on marriage and childbirth (single person survey): twelfth basic survey on birth trends).

―――― (2005), *Jinkō tōkei shiryō shū (2005-nen ban), Hyō 6–23: Seibetsu shōgai mikon ritsu oyobi shokon nenrei* (Population statistics data collection (2005 edition), Tables 6–23: Lifetime unmarried rate and age at first marriage, by sex).

―――― (2006), *Kekkon to shussan ni kansuru zenkoku chōsa (dokushin chōsa): dai-jūsan-kai shussei dōkō kihon chōsa* (Nationwide survey on marriage and childbirth (single person survey): thirteenth basic survey on birth trends).

Kolb, Judith A. (1997), 'Are we still stereotyping leadership? A look at gender and other predictors of leader emergence,' *Small Group Research*, 28, pp. 370–393.

Korea Labor Institute (2002), *KLIPS* (Korean Labor and Income Panel Study) *User's Guide*, Seoul: Korea.

Kōsei Rōdōshō (Ministry of Health, Labour and Welfare) (2003), *Heisei 15-nen kokumin seikatsu kiso chōsa* (2003 Basic Survey of National Life).

―――― (2004), *Dai-ikkai nijūisseiki shusseiji jūdan chōsa* (First national longitudinal survey on newly-born children of the twenty-first century).

——— (2005), *Dai-nikai nijūisseiki seinensha jūdan chōsa* (Second national longitudinal survey on adults of the twenty-first century).

——— (2006), *Jinkō dōtai tōkei tokushu hōkoku: shussei ni kansuru tōkei no gaikyō* (Special report on vital statistics of population: overview of birth statistics).

Kōsei Rōdōshō Koyō Kintō/Jidō Katei-kyoku (Equal Employment, Children and Families Bureau, Ministry of Health, Labour and Welfare) (ed.) (2004), *Heisei jūgo-nen ban josei rōdō hakusho: hataraku josei no jitsujō* (2003 edition white paper on female labour: the current situation of working women), Tokyo: (Zai) Nijūisseiki Shokugyō Zaidan (Japan Institute of Workers' Evolution, Inc.).

——— (ed.) (2005), *Heisei jūroku-nen ban josei rōdō hakusho: hataraku josei no jitsujō* (2004 edition white paper on female labour: the current situation of working women), Tokyo: (Zai) Nijūisseiki Shokugyō Zaidan (Japan Institute of Workers' Evolution, Inc.).

——— (ed.) (2006), *Josei rōdō no bunseki 2005-nen: chūkōnen josei no shūgyō jittai to ishiki* (Analysis of female labour, 2005: the current situation of middle-aged and older women's employment and their attitudes).

Kumazawa, Makoto (2000), *Josei rōdō to kigyō shakai* (Female labour and corporate society), Tokyo: Iwanami Shinsho.

Lee, Jaeyeol 1996 'Interrelation between production and labor and its effect on female employment,' *The Population Studies of Korea*, 19(1), pp.5–44.

Lee, Sunhwa (2001), 'Women's education, work, and marriage in South Korea,' in Mary C. Brinton (ed.), *Women's Working Lives in East Asia*, Stanford, California: Stanford University Press, pp. 204–232.

Lehrer, Evelyn, and Marc Nerlove (1986), 'Female labor force behavior and fertility in the U.S.' *Annual Review of Sociology*, 12, pp. 181–204.

Leibowitz, Arleen, Jacob Alex Klerman and Linda J. Waite (1992), 'Employment of new mothers and child care choice: differences by children's age,' *Journal of Human Resources*, 27, pp. 112–134.

Lennon, Mary Clare (1999), 'Work and Unemployment as Stressors,' in Allan V. Horwitz and Teresa L. Scheid (eds), *A Handbook for the Study of Mental Health*, New York: Cambridge University Press, pp. 284–294.

Lockheed, Marlaine E., and Katherine P. Hall (1976), 'Conceptualising sex as a status characteristic: applications to leadership training strategies,' *Journal of Social Issues*, 32, pp. 111–124.

Lord, Robert G., and Karen J. Maher (1991), *Leadership and information processing: linking perceptions and performance*, Boston, Massachusetts: Unwin Hyman.

McLanahan, Sara, and Julia Adams (1987), 'Parenthood and psychological well-being,' *Annual Review of Sociology*, 13, pp. 237–257.

Mason, Karen Oppenheim, John L. Czaika and Sara Arber (1976), 'Change in U.S. women's sex-role attitudes, 1964–1974,' *American Sociological Review*, 41(1), pp. 573–596.

Mason, Karen Oppenheim, and Karen Kohlthau (1989), 'Determinants of child care ideals among mothers of preschool-aged children,' *Journal of Marriage and the Family*, 51, pp. 593–603.

Matsuda, Shigeki (2004), 'Dansei no kaji sanka: kaji sanka o kitei suru yōin (Men's participation in household work: factors affecting participation in household work),' in Hideki Watanabe, Akihide Inaba and Naoko Shimazaki (eds), *Gendai Nihon kazoku no kōzō to hen'yō* (Structure and change in contemporary Japanese families: quantitative analyses of National Family Research (NFRJ98), Tokyo: University of Tokyo Press, pp. 175–189.

———— (2006), 'Dansei no kaji sanka no henka: NFRJ98, 03 o mochiita bunseki (A change in men's housework participation in Japan: analysis by NFRJ98 and NFRJ03),' in Michiko Nishino, Akihide Inaba and Naoko Shimazaki (eds), *Dai ni-kai zenkoku kazoku chōsa dai ni-ji hōkokusho: 1 fūfu, setai, raifu kōsu* (Working Papers of National Family Research of Japan 2003, Volume 1: wives and husbands, households, and life course), Tokyo: Nihon Kazoku Shakai Gakkai Zenkoku Kazoku Chōsa Iinkai (National Research Committee of Japan Society of Family Sociology), pp. 35–48.

Meindl, James R. (1995), 'The romance of leadership as a follower-centric theory: a social constructionist approach,' *Leadership Quarterly*, 6, pp. 329–341.

Merton, Robert K. (1968), *Social Theory and Social Structure*, enlarged ed., New York: Free Press.

Mincer, Jacob (1960), 'Employment and consumption,' *Review of Economics and Statistics,* 42(1), pp. 20–26.

Mirowsky, John, and Catherine E. Ross (1989), *Social Causes of Psychological Distress*, New York: Aldine de Gruyter.

Misumi, Jūji (1985), *The Behavioural Science of Leadership: An Interdisciplinary Japanese Research Program*, Ann Arbor, Michigan: University of Michigan Press.

Mitsuyama, Masako (2000), 'Daikyōsō jidai no Nihon no josei pāto rōdō: kokusai hikaku no shiten kara (Japanese women's part-time work in an age of great competition: from the perspective of international comparison),' in Emiko Takenaka and Yoshiko Kuba (superv. eds), *Rōdō to jendā* (Work and gender), Tokyo: Akashi Shoten, pp. 169–189.

Molm, Linda D. (1978), 'Sex role attitudes and the employment of married women: the direction of causality,' *Sociological Quarterly*, 19(4), pp. 522–533.

Montgomery, James D. (1994), 'Revisiting *Tally's Corner*: mainstream norms, cognitive dissonance, and underclass behaviour,' *Rationality and Society*, 6(4), pp. 462–488.

Nagai, Akiko (1992), 'Tomo-bataraki fūfu no kaji suikō (Household work by dual-income couples),' *Kazoku Shakaigaku Kenkyū* (Japanese Journal of Family Sociology), 4, pp. 67–77.

Naikakufu (Cabinet Office) (2002), *Heisei jūsan-nendo kokumin seikatsu hakusho* (2001–2002 white paper on national life).

———— (2004), *Dai-nana-kai sekai seishōnen ishiki chōsa: kekka gaiyō sokuhō* (Seventh world youth awareness survey: results summary bulletin).

Naikakufu Danjo Kyōdō Sankaku Kaigi (Conference for Gender Equality, Cabinet Office) (2005), *Shōshika to danjo kyōdō sankaku ni kansuru shakai kankyō no kokusai hikaku hōkokusho: gaiyō ban* (International comparative report on the social environment relating to the falling birth-rate and gender-equal participation: summary version).

Naikakufu Danjo Kyōdō Sankaku-kyoku (Gender Equality Bureau, Cabinet

Office) (ed.) (2002), *Danjo kyōdō sankaku shakai ni kansuru kokusai hikaku chōsa* (International comparative survey on a gender-equal society). *http://www.gender.go.jp/*.

―――― (2004), *Danjo kyōdō sankaku shakai ni kansuru yoron chōsa* (Public opinion poll on a gender-equal society), *http://www8.cao.go.jp/survey/h16/h16-danjo/index.html*.

Nakamura, Alice, and Masao Nakamura (1985), 'Dynamic models of the labor force behavior of married women which can be estimated using limited amounts of past information,' *Journal of Econometrics*, 27(3), pp. 273–298.

NHK Hōsō Bunka Kenkyūjo (NHK Broadcasting Culture Research Institute) (ed.) (2004), *Gendai Nihonjin no ishiki kōzō* (The structure of contemporary Japanese consciousness), sixth edition, Tokyo: Nihon Hōsō Shuppan Kyōkai.

Nihon Kazoku Shakai Gakkai Zenkoku Kazoku Chōsa Iinkai (Research Committee of National Family Research in Japan, Japan Society of Family Sociology) (ed.) (2005), *Dai ni-kai kazoku ni tsuite no zenkoku chōsa (NFRJ03)* (Second National Family Research in Japan (NFRJ03)), Tokyo: Nihon Kazoku Shakai Gakkai Zenkoku Kazoku Chōsa Iinkai.

Nihon Keizai Shimbun (2004a), 'Za choisu. Kekkon shitara tomobataraki suru ka dō ka (The choice: whether to have a dual income once married),' *Nihon Keizai Shimbun*, 15 August.

―――― (2004b), 'Shū gojūjikan ijō rōdō: Nihon, yonin ni hitori (Working fifty or more hours per week: one Japanese in four,' *Nihon Keizai Shimbun*, 28 October.

―――― (2006), 'Kankoku, shōshika taisaku ni yonchō en (Korea: four billion yen to counter falling birth-rate),' *Nihon Keizai Shimbun*, 8 June.

Nijūisseiki Shokugyō Zaidan (Japan Institute of Workers' Evolution) (2006a), *Tōkeihyō zuhyō 25 'Yakushokusha ni shimeru josei wariai no suii* (Statistical tables, Figure 25: Transitions in the proportion of women among corporate officers),' *http://www.jiwe.or.jp/jyoho/data/index.html*.

―――― (2006b), *Josei kanrishoku no ikusei to tōyō ni kansuru ankēto kekka hōkokusho* (Report on the results of a questionnaire survey relating to the fostering and recruitment of female executives), *http://www.jiwe.or.jp/jyoho/chosa/h1706kanrisyoku.html*.

Nishimura, Junko (2004), 'Ikujiki-go no josei no shūgyō to kazoku seikatsu (Women's employment and family life during the post-child-rearing stage),' in Hideki Watanabe, Akihide Inaba and Naoko Shimazaki (eds), *Gendai Nihon kazoku no kōzō to hen'yō* (Structure and change in contemporary Japanese families: quantitative analyses of National Family Research (NFRJ98)), Tokyo: University of Tokyo Press, pp. 215–230.

―――― (2005), 'Shokugyō seikatsu no kazoku seikatsu e no eikyō (The effect of work life upon family life),' *Kazoku Shakaigaku Kenkyū* (Japanese Journal of Family Sociology), 17 (1), pp. 25–33.

Ojima, Fumiaki (2000), '"Rinen" kara "nichijō" e: hen'yō suru seibetsu yakuwari bungyō ishiki (From the "ideal" to the "ordinary": changing attitudes towards gender division of labour),' in Kazuo Seiyama (ed.) *Jendā, shijō, kazoku* (Gender, market, and family), *Nihon no kaisō shisutemu* (Stratification system in Japan), vol. 4, Tokyo: University of Tokyo Press, pp. 217–236.

Opp, Karl-Dieter (1989), *The Rationality of Political Protest: A Comparative Analysis of Rational Choice Theory*, Boulder: Westview Press.

Park, Soo-Mi (2002), 'The consequences of life events on Korean women's first entry into and withdrawal from the labor market,' *Han'guk Sahoehak* (Korean Journal of Sociology), 36(2), pp. 145–174.

Phang, Hanam (1994), 'A Dynamic Study of Young Women's Labor Market Transitions over the Early Life Course: Cohort Trends, Racial Differentials, and Determinants,' unpublished Ph.D. dissertation, University of Wisconsin-Madison.

Phelps, Edmund S. (1972), 'The statistical theory of racism and sexism,' *American Economic Review*, 62(4), pp. 659–661.

Polachek, Solomon William (1978), 'Sex differences in college major,' *Industrial and Labor Relations Review*, 31(4), pp. 498–508.

Rabin, Matthew (1994), 'Cognitive dissonance and social change,' *Journal of Economic Behavior and Organization*, 23, pp. 177–194.

Ridgeway, Cecilia L. (2001), 'Gender, status, and leadership,' *Journal of Social Issues*, 57, pp. 637–655.

Ridgeway, Cecilia L., and Joseph Berger (1986), 'Expectations, legitimation, and dominance behavior in groups,' *American Sociological Review*, 51, pp. 603–617.

Riggio, Ronald E. (1986), 'Assessment of basic social skills,' *Journal of Personality and Social Psychology*, 51, pp. 649–660.

Runciman, Walter G. (1966), *Relative Deprivation and Social Justice: A Study of Attitudes to Social Inequality in Twentieth-Century England*, London: Routledge & Kegan Paul.

Sackett, Paul R., Cathy L. Z. DuBois and Ann Wiggins Noe (1991), 'Tokenism in performance evaluation: the effects of work group representation on male-female and white-black differences in performance ratings,' *Journal of Applied Psychology*, 76, pp. 263–267.

Sakamoto, Yosiyuki, Makio Ishiguro and Genshirō Kitagawa (1986) (1983), *Akaike Information Criterion Statistics*, Tokyo: KTK Scientific Publishers/ Dordrecht: D. Reidel.

Sakata, Kiriko (2002), 'Jendā sutereotaipu no sayō o kitei suru shūdan yōin no kentō (Examination of group-level factors that regulate the function of gender stereotypes),' *Heisei 12–14-nendo kagaku kenkyū seika hōkokusho* (Report on results of scientific research, 2000–2002 fiscal years), Grant-in-Aid for Scientific Research (C)(2), Project number: 12610127.

Sakata, Kiriko, and Masaru Kurokawa (1992), 'Sex differences in leader behavior from the perspective of attitudes toward sex roles and influence strategies,' *Jikken Shakai Shinrigaku Kenkyū* (Japanese Journal of Experimental Social Psychology), 31, pp. 187–202.

——— (1993), 'Chihō jichitai ni okeru shokuba no rīdāshippu kinō no seisa no kenkyū: "Jōshi no seibetsu to buka no seibetsu no kumiawase" kara no bunseki (Gender differences on leadership processes in city government organizations),' *Sangyō Soshiki Shinrigaku Kenkyū* (Japanese Association of Industrial/Organizational Psychology Journal), 7, pp. 15–23.

Sano, Sachiko, and Mitsuru Wakabayashi (1990), 'Hataraku josei no danjo byōdō ishiki: danjo koyō kintō hō sekō gonen go no jitsujō (Working women's consciousness of gender-equality: the actual situation five years after the enactment of the Equal Employment Opportunity Law),' *Keiei Kōdō Kagaku* (Japanese Journal of Administrative Science), 5, pp. 99–111.

Schein, Virginia E. (1973), 'The relationship between sex role stereotypes and requisite management characteristics,' *Journal of Applied Psychology*, 57, pp. 95–100.

—— (1975), 'Relationships between sex role stereotypes and requisite management characteristics among female managers,' *Journal of Applied Psychology*, 60, pp. 340–344.

—— (2001), 'A global look at psychological barriers to women's progress in management,' *Journal of Social Issues*, 57, pp. 675–688.

Simon, Robin W. (2002), 'Revisiting the relationship among gender, marital status and health,' *American Journal of Sociology*, 107(4), pp. 1065–1096.

Smith-Lovin, Lynn, and Ann R. Tickamyer (1978), 'Nonrecursive models of labor participation, fertility behavior and sex role attitudes,' *American Sociological Review*, 43(4), pp. 541–557.

Snyder, Mark (1974), 'Self-monitoring of expressive behaviour,' *Journal of Personality and Social Psychology*, 30, pp. 526–537.

Sōmuchō Tōkei-kyoku (Statistics Bureau, Management and Coordination Agency) (2002), *Heisei jūsan-nen shakai seikatsu kihon chōsa: seikatsu jikan ni kansuru kekka* (2001 basic survey on social life: results relating to time use in everyday life).

Sōmushō (Ministry of Internal Affairs and Communications) (2006), *Kokusei chōsa sokuhō* (National population census preliminary report).

Sōmushō Tōkei-kyoku (Statistics Bureau, Ministry of Internal Affairs and Communications) (2005), *Heisei jūnana-nendo rōdōryoku chōsa nenpō* (Annual report on the labour force survey).

Sōrifu (Prime Minister's Office) (2000), *Danjo kyōdō sankaku shakai ni kansuru yoron chōsa* (Public opinion poll on a gender-equal society).

Spence, A. Michael (1974), *Market Signalling: Information Transfer in Hiring and Related Screening Processes*, Cambridge, Massachusetts: Harvard University Press.

Spencer, Steven J., Claude M. Steele and Diane M. Quinn (1999), 'Stereotype threat and women's math performance,' *Journal of Experimental Social Psychology*, 35, pp. 4–28.

Steele, Claude M., and Joshua Aronson (1995), 'Stereotype threat and the intellectual test performance of African Americans,' *Journal of Personality and Social Psychology*, 69, pp. 797–811.

Stone, Jeff, Christian I. Lynch, Mike Sjomeling and John M. Darley (1999), 'Stereotype threat effects on Black and White athletic performance,' *Journal of Personality and Social Psychology*, 77, pp. 1213–1227.

Stouffer, Samuel A., Edward A. Suchman, Leland C. DeVinney, Shirley A. Star and Robin M. Williams (1949), *The American Soldier*, vol. 1, *Adjustment during Army Life*, Princeton: Princeton University Press.

Suemori, Kei (1999), 'Otto no kaji suikō oyobi jōcho-teki sapōto to tsuma no fūfu kankei manzoku-kan: tsuma no seibetsu yakuwari bungyō ishiki to no kōgo sayō' (Husband's participation in household work, emotional support and wife's marital satisfaction: interaction effects with attitude toward sexual division of labour),' *Kazoku Shakaigaku Kenkyū* (Japanese Journal of Family Sociology), 11, pp. 71–82.

Sung, Jaimei, and Eunyoung Chah (2000), 'Co-residence and its effect on labor supply of married women,' *Proceedings of the First Annual Meeting of Korea Labor and Income Panel Study*, pp. 62–83.

Suzuki, Atsuko (1991), 'Egalitarian sex role attitudes: scale development and comparison of American and Japanese women,' *Sex Roles*, 24, pp. 245–259.

────── (1996), 'Jakunen josei no kyaria sentaku kitei yōin ni kansuru jūdanteki kenkyū: dōitsu soshiki ni okeru shūrō keizoku oyobi tenshoku (Longitudinal study on the determinants of career choice among young women: to continue or to change jobs within the same organisation),' *Shinrigaku Kenkyū* (Japanese Journal of Psychology), 67, pp. 118–126.

────── (2004), 'Jakunen danjo no kyaria sentaku kitei yōin ni kansuru jūdanteki kenkyū: shitsumonshi chōsa (A longitudinal study on determinant factors in young men and women's career choice: a questionnaire survey),' *2002–2004-nendo kagaku kenkyū seika hōkokusho* (Research report on 2002-2004 fiscal year grants-in-aid for scientific research).

────── (2006a), 'Kyaria to jendā: shutaiteki-na kyaria hattatsu o mezashite (Career and gender: towards autonomous career development),' in Atsuko Suzuki and Keiko Kashiwagi (eds), *Jendā no shinrigaku: kokoro to kōdō e no atarashii shiza. Shinrigaku no sekai senmon hen 5* (The psychology of gender: New perspectives on mind and behaviour. World of psychology specialist editions, 5), Tokyo: Baifūkan, pp. 147–184.

────── (2006b), 'Bunka to jendā: jendā yakuwari taido no shiten kara (Culture and gender: from the perspective of gender role attitudes),' in Atsuko Suzuki and Keiko Kashiwagi (eds), *Jendā no shinrigaku: kokoro to kōdō e no atarashii shiza. Shinrigaku no sekai senmon hen 5* (The psychology of gender: New perspectives on mind and behaviour. World of psychology specialist editions, 5), Tokyo: Baifūkan, pp. 185–215.

────── (2007), 'Kazoku to jendā (Family and gender),' in Kimihiro Shiomura and Osamu Fukushima (eds), *Shakai shinrigaku gaisetsu* (Social Psychology), Kyoto: Kitaōji Shobō, pp. 148–156.

Takahashi, Masayasu, Yoshiaki Yamaguchi and Hajime Ushimaru (1998), *Soshiki to jendā* (Organisation and gender), Tokyo: Dōbunkan.

Takeishi, Emiko (2001), 'Daisotsu josei no saishūgyō no jōkyō bunseki (Situational analysis of re-employment among female university graduates),' in Akira Wakisaka and Yasunobu Tomita (eds), *Daisotsu josei no hatarakikata: josei ga shigoto o tsuzukeru toki, yameru toki* (Work modes for female university graduates: When women continue working, when women leave their jobs), Tokyo: Nihon Rōdō Kenkyū Kikō (Japan Institute of Labour), pp. 117–141.

Tallichet, Suzanne E., and Fern K. Willits (1986), 'Gender-role attitude change of young women: influential factors from a panel study,' *Social Psychology Quarterly*, 49(2), pp. 219–227.

Tanaka, Sigeto (1996), 'Sengo Nihon ni okeru seibetsu bungyō no dōtai: josei no shokuba shinshutsu to nijū no shōheki' (The changing sexual division of labour in postwar Japan: the double barrier against the employment of women), *Kazoku Shakaigaku Kenkyū* (Japanese Journal of Family Sociology), 8, pp. 151–61.

────── (1997), 'Kōgakureki-ka to seibetsu-bungyō: josei no furutaimu keizoku shūgyō ni taisuru gakkō kyōiku no kōka (Higher education and the sexual division of labour: the schooling effect on women's continuous fulltime employment),' *Shakaigaku Hyōron* (Japanese Sociological Review), 48(2), pp. 130–142.

Thibodeau, Ruth, and Elliot Aronson (1992), 'Taking a closer look: reasserting the role of the self-concept in dissonance theory,' *Personality and Social Psychology Bulletin*, 18(5), pp. 591–602.

Thoits, Peggy A. (1983), 'Multiple identities and psychological well-being: a reformulation and test of the social isolation hypothesis,' *American Sociological Review*, 48, pp. 174–187.

——— (1995), 'Stress, coping and social support processes: where are we? What next?' *Journal of Health and Social Behaviour*, Extra Issue, pp. 53–79.

Thornton, Arland, Duane F. Alwin and Donald Camburn (1983), 'Causes and consequences of sex-role attitudes and attitude change,' *American Sociological Review*, 48(2), pp. 211–227.

Thornton, Arland, and Deborah Freedman (1979), 'Changes in the sex role attitudes of women, 1962–1977: evidence from a panel study,' *American Sociological Review*, 44(5), pp. 831–842.

Treadway, Darren C., Wayne A. Hochwarter, Gerald R. Ferris, Charles J. Kacmar, Ceasar Douglas, Anthony P. Ammeter and M. Ronald Buckley (2004), 'Leader political skill and employee reactions,' *Leadership Quarterly*, 15, pp. 493–513.

Umberson, Debra, and Kristi Williams (1999), 'Family Status and Mental Health,' in Carol S. Aneshensel and Jo C. Phelan (eds), *Handbook of the Sociology of Mental Health*. New York: Kluwer Academic/ Plenum Publishers, pp. 225–253.

van-Knippenberg, Barbara, Daan van-Knippenberg, David De-Cremer and Michael A. Hogg (2005), 'Research in leadership, self, and identity: a sample of the present and a glimpse of the future,' *Leadership Quarterly*, 16, pp. 495–499.

Wakisaka, Akira (1990), *Kaisha-gata josei* (Women in the workplace), Tokyo: Dōbunkan.

Walker, Ian, and Heather J. Smith (eds) (2002), *Relative Deprivation: Specification, Development and Integration*, Cambridge: Cambridge University Press.

Watanabe, Hideki, Akihide Inaba and Naoko Shimazaki (eds) (2004), *Gendai Nihon kazoku no kōzō to hen'yō* (Structure and change in contemporary Japanese families: quantitative analyses of National Family Research (NFRJ98)), Tokyo: University of Tokyo Press.

Wenk, Deeann, and Patricia Garrett (1992), 'Having a baby: some predictions of maternal employment around childbirth,' *Gender and Society*, 6(1), pp. 49–65.

Wickens, Thomas D. (1989), *Multiway Contingency Tables Analysis for the Social Sciences*, Hillsdale, New Jersey: Lawrence Erlbaum Associates.

Yamaguchi, Kazuo (1998), 'Kieyuku shōsū-ha: shōgai mishūgyō josei no rekishiteki genshō to sono kettei yōin ni tsuite (A vanishing minority: on the historical decrease of lifetime never-employed women and its determinant factors). *Shokugyō kyaria to raifu kōsu no Nichi–Bei hikaku kenkyū: chōsa kenkyū hōkokusho* (Research report: a Japan–U.S. comparative study on work career and life course), no. 112, Tokyo: Nihon Rōdō Kenkyū Kikō (Japan Institute of Labour), pp. 19–51.

——— (1999), 'Kikon josei no seibetsu yakuwari ishiki to shakai kaisō: Nihon to Beikoku no kyōtsūsei to ishitsusei ni tsuite (Married women's gender-role attitudes and social stratification: Commonalities and differences between Japan and the U.S.A.),' *Shakaigaku Hyōron* (Japanese Sociological Review), 50, pp. 231–252.

Yamato, Reiko (2006), 'Otto no kaji ikuji sanka wa tsuma no fūfu kankei manzoku-do o takameru ka?: koyō fukyō jidai ni okeru kaji ikuji buntan no yukue (Does husbands' sharing of housework and child-rearing increase wives' marital satisfaction under the economic recession in the 1990s to the 2000s in Japan?),' in Michiko Nishino, Akihide Inaba and Naoko Shimazaki (eds), *Dai ni-kai zenkoku kazoku chōsa dai ni-ji hōkokusho: 1 fūfu, setai, raifu kōsu* (Working papers of national family research of Japan 2003 Volume 1: wives and husbands, households, and life course), Tokyo: Nihon Kazoku Shakai Gakkai Zenkoku Kazoku Chōsa Iinkai (National Research Committee of Japan Society of Family Sociology), pp. 17–33.

Yee, Jaeyeol (1996), 'Interrelation between production and reproduction labor, and its effect on female employment,' *Han'gukin'guhak* (Population Studies of Korea), 19(1), pp. 5–44.

Yoder, Janice D. (2001), 'Making leadership work more effectively for women,' *Journal of Social Issues*, 57, pp. 815–828.

Zaccaro, Stephen J., Roseanne J. Foti and David A. Kenny (1991), 'Self-monitoring and trait-based variance in leadership: an investigation of leader flexibility across multiple group situations,' *Journal of Applied Psychology*, 76, pp. 308–315.

Index

ageing society, 7, 110
agency, 43, 63, 69–70
Angel Plan, 142
aspiration, 7, 68, 84, 92–101, 103, 105–107
  educational, 84, 92–101, 103, 105–107
  work/career, 95–97, 107
average life expectancy, 3–4, 7

Bakan, David, 63
Basic Law for a Gender-Equal Society, 9, 38
Becker, Gary S., 70–71, 86, 114, 117
Bem, Sandra M., 69–70
Berger, Joseph M., 62, 66
Brinton, Mary C., 84, 89, 92, 102, 147, 149

care services, 3, 23, 57
  provision of care services for ill children, 57
career development, 1, 3, 14, 19, 22–25, 28, 31
career-interruption, 130–133, 143
censored data, 126–127
Center for Epidemiological Studies Depression Scale, 41
child-care 6, 9, 14–20, 23–26, 35, 54, 57, 128–129, 131, 133–139
  leave, 9, 17–20, 23–25
  services, 23
Child-care and Family-care Leave Law, 9

child-rearing, 5, 13, 18–19, 23, 25, 32–41, 43, 45, 47–57, 59, 111–114, 116–120, 123–125, 130, 133, 137, 139–140
childbirth, 33, 35, 59, 92, 94–95, 110–114, 117–143
children's day-care centres, 36
cognitive dissonance, 84, 93–95, 98, 100–103, 106, 147–149
communion, 63, 69, 71
Cox's proportional hazard model, 126–127, 136

daily role, 56
declining birth-rate, 3, 5, 32
declining fertility, 5, 13, 31
dekichatta kekkon, 6
discrimination, 8–9, 13, 21, 92, 94, 112, 114–115
distress, 14, 33, 37, 41, 44–48, 50–54, 56
  psychological, 12, 33, 37, 41, 45–46, 50–51, 56
division of labour, 2, 10–11, 16–17, 19–20, 22, 28, 31, 33, 36, 38, 55–56, 75, 84, 86, 90, 92–93, 95–97, 100, 149
dual labour market theory, 115

Eagly, Alice H., 60–66, 68, 82
education, 2, 4, 9–11, 15, 21, 24, 27, 30, 44, 48, 51–52, 62–63, 70–71, 82, 84–109, 112, 115, 118, 121, 125, 133, 137, 140, 146–148 *See also* higher education

165

educational economics, 86, 90, 92–93
egalitarian gender-role attitudes, 28–29
emergency assistance, 43, 48–54, 56
employment, 4–5, 7–17, 19–21, 23, 25–26, 32, 34–35, 39, 41, 44–47, 49–50, 53, 56–58, 84–109, 112–113, 115–126, 128–132, 134, 136–139, 141–148
  full-time, 19–20, 29, 33, 75, 86–88, 94, 128–129, 131–138, 146, 148
  part-time, 10, 16, 19–20, 29, 87–89, 94, 116, 128–129, 132–134, 136, 138, 143, 148
Equal Employment Opportunity Law, 9, 13, 58, 147
expectation-states theory, 62–63, 65, 68, 72, 75
extended family, 36

family identity, 3
family-friendly companies, 38
female executives, 10, 22, 58
female labour, 13, 19, 110, 112–114, 116–118, 139–140, 142–143
female labour force/workforce, 110, 116, 118, 139–140, 143
female workers, 9, 14, 19–20, 138, 143
feminisation of employment, 9
feminist viewpoint, 116
fertility, 5–6, 13–14, 31, 38, 110
  below-replacement fertility, 38

GEM (Gender Empowerment Measure), 28
gender
  congeniality, 64, 80
  disparity, 28, 82
  equality, 8, 26, 28, 30, 75
  gap, 15, 24
  identity, 69, 72–74
  ideology, 84–87, 89–95, 97–107, 145, 148–149 *See also* gender-role attitudes
  norms, 2, 14, 31, 74, 79
  roles, 8, 31, 72–73, 75, 113–114, 117
  stereotypes, 63, 68, 73–74, 82, 89
gender-equal society, 9, 38, 40, 54 *See also* Basic Law for a Gender-Equal Society
gender-equalisation, 34, 37–38, 40, 56
gender-inequality, 33, 112
gender-role attitudes, 2, 28–29, 31, 145–146
gender-specialisation, 116
gendered division of labour, 2, 10–11, 16–17, 19–20, 22, 28, 31, 33, 36, 38, 55–56, 75, 84, 86, 90, 92–93, 95–97, 100–101, 149
gendered wage disparity, 21
glass ceiling, 60

Hakim, Catherine, 117–120, 145–147
Hara, Junsuke, 8, 30, 86, 90, 102
higher education, 4, 27, 86, 89–90, 92–94, 101–103, 146–148
housewifisation, 8, 30

Index

human capital, 86, 90–91, 93, 100, 116, 137, 139

Inaba, Akihide, 33, 35–37, 40, 49, 55
income gap, 10
industrial reserve forces, 116
influence strategies/tactics, 60

Kim, Jikyung, 110, 117–119, 122, 124
Kimura, Kunihiro, 84, 97
kin network, 36–38
Klerman, Jacob A., 114, 117, 120–121, 123–125
Korea Labor and Income Panel Study (KLIPS), 125–126, 157

labour
  market segmentation theory, 115
  segmented market, 84, 93–95, 98, 101–103, 106, 115, 148
  supply, 113–114, 122, 124–125, 133, 139–140
labour-force participation rate, 8, 16–18, 110–112
labour-supply
  cost, 117
  decision-making, 121
leader, 59–83
leadership
  behaviour, 60–63, 65–67, 69–70, 72–74, 76–79, 81–82
  effectiveness, 58–65, 67–71, 73–75, 77–83
  style, 65, 67
Leibowitz, Arleen, 114, 120–121, 123–125

life career, 1–2, 12, 31–32
life-course, 2–4, 16–17, 24, 98–99, 102, 147, 149

M-curve, 17, 142
M-shaped structure, 111, 142
macro perspective, 1, 10
marital satisfaction, 14, 37
marriage
  bar, 94, 147
  market, 89–90, 92–93, 100, 102, 147
maternity leave, 118, 126, 134–135, 141
mental health, 12, 14, 35–36, 60, 67
micro perspective, 1
Mincer, Jacob, 113–114
motherhood protection, 140
multiple roles, 14–15

neoclassical economic theory, 113
New Angel Plan, 142
NFRJ03, 34, 40–44, 46, 48, 52, 145
NFRJ98, 34–35, 37, 40–44, 46, 48, 51, 145
nursing leave, 37, 56–57

parental leave, 38
participation in household work, 33, 35–39, 42, 47–48, 51–53, 55–57
part-time employment, 19
patriarchal system, 116–117

rational choice, 84, 93–95, 98, 100–104, 106, 147
rationalisation, 86, 89, 92–93, 100

re-employment, 17, 22–23, 141, 143–144
re-entry into the labour market, 122, 133
regularly-employed, 33–41, 44–45, 47–57
regularly-employed wife, 40, 50
relationship-oriented behaviour, 61, 67, 70, 73–74
relative deprivation, 147–149
reservation wage, 113–114, 124
return to the labour market, 113, 119–130, 133, 135–141, 143
rigid society, 22
role, 1–4, 6, 8, 9, 13–15, 29, 31, 34–35, 39, 47, 53–56, 59–61, 63, 65–73, 75–76, 78, 82–83, 116–117,
role-captivity, 35
role-expansion, 34, 39, 47
role-overload, 34–35, 39, 47, 56
role-strain, 35

Sakata, Kiriko, 58, 75–77
Seiyama, Kazuo, 8, 30, 102
self-employed, 41, 45, 87–89
self-monitoring, 69–70
self-realisation, 1–2, 4, 17, 24–25, 27
SESRA (Scale of Egalitarian Sex Role Attitudes), 29
sex segregation, 20–21
signalling, 86, 90–91, 93, 100
social role theory, 62–63, 65–68, 70, 72–73, 75, 82
social skills, 69, 71–74
social-selection, 35
socialisation, 89, 92, 149
SSM (Social Stratification and Social Mobility)

Survey, 24, 60, 63–64, 77, 85–86, 88–89, 97, 103–106, 108–109, 146
statistical discrimination, 94, 114–115
stereotype threat, 68, 74
support, 3, 5, 9, 11, 13, 18–19, 24, 26, 37, 39–40, 43–45, 47–56, 60, 68, 80, 90, 95103, 106, 120, 122, 124, 133, 137, 139–140, 148
   expressive, 37, 40, 44, 50, 53, 55–56
   instrumental, 40
   parental, 43, 54–55
   social, 37
   spousal, 37, 40
Suzuki, Atsuko, 1–2, 4, 7, 10, 12–13, 15, 24–25, 27–32

task-oriented behaviour, 61, 66, 74
total fertility rate, 5, 110
Type II error, 57, 145

wage gap, 21
Wakisaka, Akira, 89–90
well-being, 33–36, 38–41, 44–45, 47, 54, 56
withdrawal from the labour market, 118–119, 121–122, 124
women's employment-life patterns, 117
women's work-career, 110
work career, 1–3, 23, 58, 90, 93, 95–97, 105–107, 111–113
work/life balance, 2, 11, 13–14, 26, 31

Yes tendency, 42

Stratification and Inequality Series
The Center for the Study of Social Stratification and Inequality,
Tohoku University, Japan
Volume 6

Gender and Career in Japan